T5-AGL-354

WITHDRAWN
No longer the property of the
Boston Public Library.
Sale of this material benefits the Library.

18⁰⁰ 55P

TURBO GENEALOGY

The Computer-Enhanced "how-to-find-your-roots" Handbook

1987/88 edition

John C. Cosgriff Jr. and Carolyn H. Cosgriff

Progenesys Press
Christiansburg, VA 24068-2623

Copyright 1987 by John Cornelius Cosgriff, Jr., and Carolyn Cosgriff.
1987/88 Revised Edition.
(former editions entitled: *CLIMB IT RIGHT--a high-tech genealogy primer*)
Printed by Closson Press, Apollo, Pennsylvania; in the United States of America.

All rights reserved.

No part of this book may be reproduced or transmitted in any form or by any means, electronic or mechanical, including photocopying, recording, or by any information storage and retrieval system without written permission from the authors, except for the inclusion of brief quotations in a review.

ISBN 0-917255-04-6 Softcover
ISBN 0-917255-05-4 Hardcover

Library of Congress Cataloging-in-Publication Data

Cosgriff, John Cornelius.
  Turbo genealogy.

  Rev. ed. of: Climb it right. c1986.
  Bibliography: p.
  Includes index.
  1. Genealogy. 2. United States--Genealogy--
Handbooks, manuals, etc. I. Cosgriff, Carolyn H.
II. Cosgriff, John Cornelius. Climb it right.
III. Title.
CS16.C67 1987   929'.1   87-9882
ISBN 0-917255-05-4
ISBN 0-917255-04-6 (soft)

CS16
.C67
1987
copy 2

rec.
Jan. 12, 1989

Order from:
PROGENESYS PRESS
PO Box 2623
Christiansburg, VA 24068
Price, $17.95 for softcover edition; $27.95 for hardcover edition;
and $4.95 for a 1987 *Update* for those with an earlier edition.

TABLE OF CONTENTS

INTRODUCTION..5
CREDITS...6
CHAPTER 1. GETTING STARTED. FORMS AND FAMILY.....................7
    Forms..7
    Recording & Documentation; Obtaining Information from Your Relatives..........8
    Make A Family Album; Family Traditions, Summary..............................10
CHAPTER 2. THE LDS GENEALOGICAL LIBRARY............................11
    Name-Extraction & the International Genealogical Index (IGI)..................11
    Catalogs and Loan System..13
    Family Registry, GSU Research Aids...14
    AIS Indexes; the Ancestral File and Personal Ancestral File..................15
    New & Developing Resources; Summary..16
CHAPTER 3. NOTE-KEEPING AND ORGANIZATION............................17
    Record-keeping Criteria; Record-keeping Suggestions..........................17
    A Suggested Filing System...19
    What to Include in Your Notes...21
    Summary..22
CHAPTER 4. COMPUTERIZATION...23
    Introduction: Are you suited for computers; are they suited to you?..........23
    Needed Background; How Computers Work...24
    A Basic Computer System & Buying Recommmendations; Advances in Memory/Storage....25
    Benefits of Computerization...26
    Software, Including Current Genealogy Software.................................27
    Non-Genealogy Software & Industry Standards (ASCII & GEDCOM)...................29
    Shareware--A Free Software Learning Tool..30
    Computer-Genealogy Periodicals & Related Books.................................32
    User and Interest Groups for Help & Support....................................33
    Telecommunications and Modems...34
    Additional Consumer Guidelines..35
    Summary..36
CHAPTER 5. CHOOSING A LINE TO RESEARCH................................37
    Language; Distance; Available Records...37
    Mobility; Social Status; Uncooperative Family & Family Myths..................38
    Duplication...39
    Common Names; Summary...40
CHAPTER 6. USING LIBRARIES...41
    How-To's of Library Research (Card Catalog)....................................41
    (Call Number; Indexes; Targetted Approach).....................................42
    Library Genealogy Bibliographies; Obtaining Information from Other Libraries....43
    Scholarly Micropublishing; Automated Developments in Library Research..........44
    Summary..46
CHAPTER 7. COMPILED SOURCES, SOCIETIES & MAGAZINES...............47
    Genealogies and Family Histories; Local Histories.............................47
    Biographical Works; Compiled Registers & Directories;.........................48
    Local Historical Societies/Magazines, Genealogy Magazines....................48
    Newspapers..49
    Genealogical Columns; Summary; BIBLIOGRAPHY:...................................50
    (1). Bibliographies & Indexes...50
    (2). Periodical Indexes to Find Family History Articles.......................51
    (3). Newspaper Bibliographies & Indexes..52
CHAPTER 8. EVALUATION AND EVIDENCE......................................53
    Judging Printed Sources; Evidence...53
    How to Judge Conflicting Facts..55
    Safeguards when Using Circumstantial Evidence..................................55

Dating Analysis. 56
Summary. 57
CHAPTER 9. FORMULATING YOUR RESEARCH PLAN. 58
Facts Needed; Examples: Learning Specific Places/Times. 59
Defining Your Goals. 60
Example: An Analysis to Make up a Research Plan. 61
Summary. 62
CHAPTER 10. GAINING HISTORICAL, GEOGRAPHICAL BACKGROUND. 62
Geography. 63
History. 63
Learning about Records through Local Research Guides. 65
Jurisdictions. 65
Summary; BIBLIOGRAPHY: (1). Geographical Tools. 66
(2). Guides for a Number of Countries; (3). Ethnic and National Guidebooks. . . . 69
CHAPTER 11. VITAL RECORDS: GOVERNMENT, CHURCH, CEMETERY. 71
Government Vital Records. 71
Church Vital Records. 71
Cemetery Records. 73
Other Sources for Vital Statistics; Summary. 74
CHAPTER 12. COURT, LAND AND CENSUS RECORDS. 76
Court Records. 77
Land Records. 78
Census Records. 80
Summary. 82
CHAPTER 13. MILITARY, NATURALIZATION, & IMMIGRATION RECORDS. . . . 83
Military Records. 83
Naturalization Records. 84
Immigration Records. 86
Immigration List BIBLIOGRAPHY. 87
Summary. 88
CHAPTER 14. RECORD INTERPRETATION: NAMES; SPELLING; LEGALITIES; ETC. . . . 89
Names. 89
Using Names and Other Evidence for Identification. 91
Spelling Problems and Helps. 93
Meaning Changes. 94
Age, Tax, and Gender Requirements. 95
Handwriting; Summary. 96
CHAPTER 15. CORRESPONDENCE AND ADDRESSES. 97
Productive Corresondence. 97
Helpful Address Sources, Addresses of Large Some American Collections. 98
Large Genealogical Publishers/Bookstores in USA; Foreign Addresses. . . . 101
(Africa; No. & So. America; Central & E. Europe). 102
(Far East). 103
(Mid-East; Misc.; Scandinavia). 104
(Western Europe); Sample Letters (to a County Clerk, Librarian). . . . 106
(to a Relative); A Note Re: Writing County Clerks. 107
Lists of Professional Researchers; Summary. 108
APPENDIX A. RESEARCH PROCEDURE DIAGRAM. 109
APPENDIX B. SUBJECT HEADING CHECKLIST. 110
APPENDIX C. 1752 CALENDAR CHANGE. 111
APPENDIX D. REGIONAL BRANCHES, NATIONAL ARCHIVES. . . 111
APPENDIX E. LEGAL TERMS USED IN WILL AND LAND RECORDS. . . 112
APPENDIX F. SOME USA GENEALOGIAL PERIODICALS. 114
APPENDIX G. GLOSSARY: SELECTED COMPUTER/TECHNICAL TERMS. . . . 115
APPENDIX H. NEW LDS FORMS: PEDIGREE CHART & FAMILY GROUP CHART. . . . 119, 125
INDEX. 121

INTRODUCTION

If you are new to computer-genealogy, you will be pleased to know that times have never been better. The application of technology to family research has reached the point where many of our wildest and most exciting dreams are becoming realities.

Advances in the field of information storage and retrieval almost daily create new possibilities for us. Likewise, almost daily, new tools are becoming available in the field of genealogy to help us surmount many of our research challenges. Things are happening so fast in this age of information that staying current is almost impossible. Hence, the need for a volume such as this.

Of course, we couldn't help you stay up-to-date in such a fast-moving area unless we revised frequently. In addition, we now provide separate, frequent *Updates* for your previous volumes so they can remain current as well (details on order-form at end of book).

It may interest first-time readers, by the way, to know some of the topics which have, in past editions, generated the most enthusiastic reader response:

o *huge computerized databases containing well over a hundred million names and related data; free and locally accessible.*

o *family facts accumulated in 1.5 million microfilmed rolls of international records; available throughout this, and many other, countries.*

o *easy- and economical-to-use online sources.*

o *updated, low-priced and free research guides for all states, most countries and ethnic groups.*

o *necessary whys, whens, whats, and hows to successfully computerize family research. This includes knowing how to choose the best computers and software (including valuable "freeware").*

But there is more than just keeping abreast of current happenings in computer-genealogy and information technology. Regardless of all of today's excellent advances; successful research must still be based upon a strong, solid, and in many ways traditional, foundation. Thus, as in previous editions (appearing under the title (*CLIMB IT RIGHT--a high-tech genealogical primer*) our objective remains the same:

> **Our goal is to help you bridge the gap between time-proven research principles of the past, and time-saving, research-expanding approaches of the present.**

Many changes have occurred in the almost one year since our last edition. To stay current, we have made extensive additions and changes, especially in Chapter 4 and, to a lesser extent, in Chapter 2. (Note here yet another electronic age benefit. Through computer-aided self-publishing we can quickly update and get new information to you, without the long delays inherent in traditional book publishing.)

As always, we not only welcome, but solicit your suggestions on how we can improve this work for you in each succeeding edition. While doing all that we can to update our facts each time we go to press, yet there is always the possibility of error. *We thus offer a free copy of our next revised edition if you will bring a content error to our attention prior to our next press time, or if you can add a source of help we think should be included.* (See details on order-form at end of book.)

Lastly, we are confident in wishing each of you much success in this, the most intriguing of adventures: the search for roots!

CREDITS

While we assume full responsibility for viewpoints expressed, as well as for any errors which may not have been uncovered prior to publication; yet we wish to publicly express our deeply-felt appreciation to the many people whose efforts, suggestions, help, and kind consideration made posible the quick completion of this project.

Special thanks go to P. William Filby, genealogical author, editor, and, (especially) "encourager"; Bill Johnson, former editor of the *Roots* Users-Group newsletter; Paul and Sara Andereck of *Genealogical Computing*; Bob and Joanne Posey of Posey International; Steve Vorenburg and Bill Mitchell of *Quinsept*; Richard Pence, editor of the *NGS Computer Interest Group Digest*; A. Gregory Brown and Bob Foster of the Genealogical Library of the Church of Jesus Christ of Latter-day Saints; Howard Nurse and Ken Whitaker of Commsoft; and Peggy Field, present President of the NGS CIG.

Charles Hoster, International Liason Offier of the NGS, and Dr. John T. Golden, editor of the *Palatine Immigrant* and expert on German and Irish sources, provided especially valuable aid in helping us compile the updated addresses found in Chapter 15. Dorothy V. Russell, editor of *Western Maryland Genealogy*, provided us with further address and other corrections. Others who assisted were friends James and Cherie Hassall of H & H Computer Enterprises; Connie Meredith, fellow author and genealogist; Ann Holberton, our local DAR resource; Pat Johnson, historian par excellence; and Glenn Lowry, former Systems' Librarian at Virginia Tech. Numerous students, friends and family have also both taught and encouraged us along the way. Our sister Diane Showalter arranged for the cover artwork.

Finally, we extend deserved recognition to our esteemed parents and children: John C. and Erma Cosgriff; Bill and Betty Read; Kimberly, Candice, Joseph Casey, Rachel Lynn, Grant Jeremy, Leslie Elizabeth and Samantha Kory. Their patience, help, and occasional (justified) complaints, buoyed us up, or brought us back down, depending on which we needed. To them--our past and our future--we dedicate this book.

Chapter 1. GETTING STARTED: FORMS AND FAMILY

> Other chapters will detail the excellent advantages related to conducting research in an "age of information." But there are initial and ongoing challenges that remain unchanged. These consist of (1) organizing family facts already known; (2) gaining more information; and (3) ensuring accuracy throughout.

These challenges are actually related. Good organization often suggests your next research steps; concern for accuracy motivates seeking out all relevant sources; these, in turn, often yield yet further facts to help your research progress.

A good beginning step, therefore, is to organize your presently-known family data by recording it onto appropriate forms. As a visual reference, they help you both as you *plan* and then *implement* your research. Keep them accurate and updated throughout your research, then, to proceed more logically. Some genealogical software allows the printing out of a variety of helpful forms. But we need to begin by examining the two most basic:.

FORMS

The *Pedigree* Chart traces one line back for several generations. The *Family Group* Chart gives data on just one couple and their children. Appendix H shows the revised versions of these forms introduced by the Genealogical Society of the Church of Jesus Christ of Latter-Day Saints, April, 1987. Reproduce these if you like, or obtain copies free or at cost through the library of any local LDS Church (find their number under the "Churches" listing in your yellow-pages). There are other, more expensive, versions available that some may prefer (e.g., fold-out pedigree charts to record up to fifteen generations).

On the pedigree chart, entry #1 is yourself or another whose direct line you wish to record. #2 is the father, and #3 is the mother of #1; #4 is the father, and #5 the mother of #2; this pattern is followed throughout. That is, an even number twice as great as the child's always belongs to the father; with the next higher, odd, number belonging to the mother. By making use of the notation, "No. 1 on this chart is the same as no.___ on chart no.___ ," it's possible to extend any line as far back as desired, through using multiple charts.

The family group charts provide complete vital facts regarding one couple and all their known children. For extra-large families, or prior or later marriages, use additional sheets, attached to the first, to include that information. *To begin your research fill out a pedigree chart, and then the appropriate family group charts for every couple on your pedigree chart.*

As use of these family group charts suggests, your research will be most productive when you make it your goal to *obtain information on complete families*, rather than just individuals. Even if just interested in your direct line (i.e. parents, grandparents, great-grandparents, etc.), yet clues about them often come only as you learn about other family members. Indeed, some particularly elusive ancestors may even require extending your search to include relations besides just siblings. If you learn of facts besides just those standard designated fields on the charts, record this miscellany in some unused space.

> Look in every possible source of information. This will not only check against facts you already have; it will often uncover details not found elsewhere.

RECORDING and DOCUMENTATION

Keep the information neat enough to be readable without spending valuable time re-writing or re-typing. You can easily add to or change your facts, as well as make your own forms, with the good genealogical software detailed in Chapter 4. But even without this time-saving advantage, do what it takes to keep your family charts accurate, updated, and in good good order, so that you can examine and analyze all relevant family facts together.

To help ensure accuracy while filling out these forms, as well as in later recording research notes, it is necessary to *carefully document the source of each fact separately* when obtaining it. Do this by appending a superscript number (first fact[1], second fact[2], third fact[3], etc.) to each fact when recording it into its appropriate field. This same number is then put into the lower left-hand "source of information" field, followed by a complete description of the source containing this fact, as below illustrated. Knowing the source of a fact is necessary to properly evaluate its worth (see Chapter 8). It is also important to be able to go back and recheck this source if needed, e.g., if conflicting data is later found.

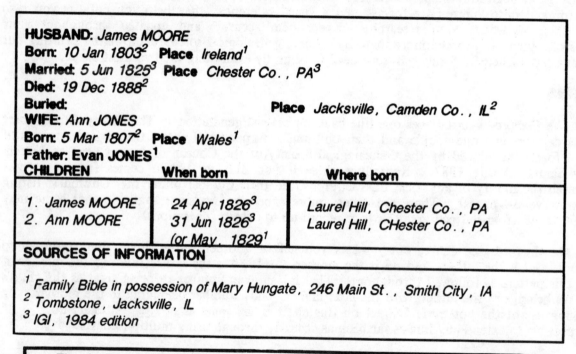

HUSBAND: *James MOORE*
Born: *10 Jan 1803[2]*   **Place** *Ireland[1]*
Married: *5 Jun 1825[3]*   **Place** *Chester Co., PA[3]*
Died: *19 Dec 1888[2]*
Buried: **Place** *Jacksville, Camden Co., IL[2]*
WIFE: *Ann JONES*
Born: *5 Mar 1807[2]*   **Place** *Wales[1]*
Father: *Evan JONES[1]*

CHILDREN	When born	Where born
1. *James MOORE*	*24 Apr 1826[3]*	*Laurel Hill, Chester Co., PA*
2. *Ann MOORE*	*31 Jun 1826[3]*	*Laurel Hill, CHester Co., PA*
	(or May, 1829[1])	

SOURCES OF INFORMATION

[1] *Family Bible in possession of Mary Hungate, 246 Main St., Smith City, IA*
[2] *Tombstone, Jacksville, IL*
[3] *IGI, 1984 edition*

Fig. 1. Example of documentation excerpted from a family group chart

OBTAINING INFORMATION FROM YOUR RELATIVES

Few can proceed back very far on the basis of their own information. You next want to contact family members. Begin by talking with close relatives, but you'll also want to reach out to more distant cousins as you learn about them. For most, the family network will be your most productive source of information, at least in the beginning. And for some of you it will continue to be for a good long time. Not only is it easier to learn your family history from those with some personal knowledge of it, but is also generally far more interesting. From relatives you can learn the anecdotes and personalities in a way seldom possible from public records.

It is especially important to gain information from relatives regarding the most recent generations of your family. Governmental, and other, agencies often won't release records made within the last 75 to 100 years, regarding them as confidential. Learn just as much as you can from relatives, then, before doing anything else. It is best, of course, to begin by talking to the oldest in your family. Don't put it off. Besides usually having the greatest family knowledge, they are also most likely to die soonest; often taking a veritable storehouse of family genealogical treasure into the grave with them. Sometimes the most elderly may be suffering with various degrees of senility. Even then, however, your attempts to help them recall early memories will often be both rewarded and rewarding.

Oral interviewing has recently received the serious attention of scholars and historians. At least two helpful guidelines have emerged: *show genuine interest*, and *relate your questions personally to the person interviewed*. Doing so will help your interviewee feel at ease, and generally result in more productive and enjoyable sessions for both of you.

To obtain the desired death date of somebody's parent, for example, start by asking questions about the interviewee's life. As you both grow comfortable, ask such relevant questions as, "How old were *you*," or "where were *you* living when your father/mother died?" Tape-record your information, if possible, but it is safest to make back-up notes as well, particularly of mentioned names or places unfamiliar to you. Later in the interview, return to these to learn further details. Such an indirect approach will usually work better than merely requesting the "facts."

Keep in mind that you can seldom obtain all desired information in just one visit. And, especially if a long time since someone has talked with them about their past, the may claim not to remember a thing. Don't let such a comment deter you. Here are a few ideas:

One friend of ours simply re-visited her grandfather. In four consecutive sessions, using the same set of questions, she elicited new memories each time. Another friend, dealing with impatient and uncooperative parents ("I don't remember," or "That's not important"), enjoyed a break-through by directing family questions to her cooperative in-laws, when they happened to visit at the same time as her parents. Her parents then began to actually volunteer facts they hadn't earlier been willing to divulge. Others may want to bring a friend or relative to reminisce about "the good old days." (Use a tape, or video tape to record such valuable sessions for posterity.)

After your interview be sure to ask about any heirlooms, old photos, newspaper clippings, albums, momentos, journals, letters, and anecdotes or stories they may have or know about. Some of these visual reminders may help jog a memory. Others should provide proof or clues as to dates, places, and relationships. Yet others may provide fascinating glimpses into the lives, times, and personalities of your ancestors. If you bring a camera along, you will be able to photograph any photographs or artifacts so uncovered.

You'll soon find out, if you don't yet know, which relatives are interested in the family history. They, of course, are the ones with whom you'll want to work closely. Most will be pleased to share the work-load, and family history is always more fun and easier to accomplish when several are cooperating. Ideally, all can share their various talents.

Planning and executing family reunions, for instance, is a project to encourage. These provide excellent opportunities for interested family members to effectively plan and coordinate research, as well as to share findings. And any efforts awakening an interest in their heritage among other family members are sure to be rewarded.

> "Given society's accelerating frustrations and complexities, I wish more families would consider the strengthening tonic of reunions." —Alex Haley

MAKE A FAMILY ALBUM

Realizing how thrilled and benefitted you would be by the discovery of an ancester's journal, photo album, or family history; why not make your own contribution to present and future generations? Here's an easy way:

o   Assemble the pedigree and family group charts as they are filled out.
o   Add personal and family memorabalia, such as pictures, journals, and documents.
o   Place in a family album.
o   Put the album where all can peruse and enjoy (and copies of everything in a safe-deposit box).

(The Annex, PO Box 768, Spanish Fork, Utah, 84660 is an economical source of supplies if you want something fancier; especially for families with young children.)

FAMILY TRADITIONS

If you have ever played the parlor game "gossip," you'll know how easy it is for a statement to become distorted or changed when passed from person to person. This happens just as frequently when genealogical statements pass from generation to generation. A later chapter will detail how to check out the validity of facts you are now gathering. In the meantime, however, keep your mind open enough to follow up all clues you are now assembling; yet, at the same time, develop a healthy dose of counter-balancing skepticism (which you may want to keep to yourself to avoid offending those relatives who put great stock in them.)

Be particularly wary of family traditions of the far-fetched or "too-good-to-be-true" variety (descent from royalty, a famous historical figure, an "Indian princess," or a Mayflower immigrant) or even the common "three immigrant brothers". Although it may be tempting to begin research with a presumed famous ancestor, such attempts are almost always counter-productive. Make it a policy, rather, to work from the present, backward, one generation at a time; and to substantiate each link with well-documented preponderance of evidence, if not legal proof. By thus proceeding back in a logical, careful, and systematic manner, you should yet enjoy the opportunity to rigorously check out the intriguing possibilities now emerging from your family interviews.

In the case where extensive family research has already been conducted, do some "spot-checking" of that work by obtaining a few of the references given. By carefully comparing the original records with the facts supposed to have been derived from them, you'll soon learn how well that research was conducted, and whether any needs to be redone.

SUMMARY

Obtain pedigree and family group sheets. Next, fill them out using what you know and are able to learn from family members, recording the source of each fact. Then get together with all branches of your family. Be genuinely enthusiastic and interested in the history of each person and their forebears.

Other possibilities include visiting with, and recording memories of, the old-timers; collecting and organizing the family memorabilia; and helping with family reunions. And don't be surprised, as you spark the interest of both young and old in the family, to see a greater love and unity grow among the generations, a result few other activities can boast.

Chapter 2. LDS GENEALOGICAL LIBRARY

Now that you are organized and knowledgeable in family lore, you may profit from using the excellent tools developed by the Genealogical Society of Utah (*GSU*), owned and operated by the Church of Jesus Christ of Latter-day Saints (LDS or *Mormon* Church). This Church teaches that Heavenly Father would like all his children "sealed" as eternal family units. These sealings are based on genealogical research and performed in LDS temples. The GSU thus includes a large library system with several collections helpful to the genealogist:

1. *Published materials* (family histories, maps, references and other compiled sources).

2. *Oral genealogies* of those groups preserving their heritage through an oral tradition (as exemplified in Alex Haley's *Roots*). In a recent effort, tribal genealogists were contacted and many persuaded to tape-record the memorized genealogies.

3. *Original records* (such as civil and church). It is estimated they have already microfilmed more than 15% of the world's relevant written records. Some 1.5 million rolls are in their collection, and more than 100 microfilm cameras continue this work by adding some 40 million pages from over 40 countries yearly. Once cataloged, most microfilms are duplicated and made available for public use in both the main and branch libraries.

4. *Computerized databases*. These are useful resource files that for the last few years have been issued on computer-output-microfiche (COM). These are 4" by 6" film-like cards; each fiche containing up to 20,000 indexed names and accompanying data. The COM collections presently include the library's catalog, the names of some 125 million deceased persons, and names of almost 200,000 living researchers.

The GSU has long been on the forefront of using technology in their genealogical collections. Certainly their most ambitious project to date, however (and likely the most ambitious genealogical project ever!), is the long-term development of an advanced mainframe *Genealogical Information System* (*GIS*) to include most of the present (as well as future additional) computerized databases. During 1986 two test components of the system were used by patrons of the Main (Salt Lake) Library. That prototype proved successful. Further development and testing continues; if this too is successful, then the first public appearance of the GIS may be about 1988.

Not only will the GIS contain much more information than is presently available within the separate systems, but there will also be considerable cross-referencing. Great care is going into making this system as easy to use ("*user-friendly*") as possible.

5. *Main Library* in Salt Lake City, Utah; well over 700 *branch genealogical libraries* as of early 1987; and over 200 smaller *satellite* libraries. Most are in North America, but some are in 40 other countries. Obtain address and hours of the branch library closest to you by contacting your local LDS Church, or by writing the GSU for a current listing for your area. Through these branch libraries you can access the published and original microfilmed records of the main library through loan and photocopy services. You also have direct access to COM copies of the computerized databases found in the main library. We will now detail these.

NAME-EXTRACTION and the INTERNATIONAL GENEALOGICAL INDEX (IGI)

For many years now the GSU has successfully used a volunteer name-extraction program. Volunteers *extract*, or copy down, genealogical information from microfilmed copies of original vital records. That information is then keyed into a large computer system and contributes to the database indexed by the *International Genealogical Index*, or *IGI*. For more than a decade now, ten million names per year have thus been added to the IGI database.

The COM edition of the IGI has been updated every three years since its initial 1975 edition. But, as we go to press, it is still uncertain when the next update will appear. That's because the growing size of the IGI makes it increasingly difficult and time-consuming to issue in microfiche (this, in fact, being one of the reasons for developing the GIS).

The 1984 edition, therefore, may be around for awhile. It contains some 88 million names on some 6,700 microfiche, representing some 90 countries. England accounts for the highest percentage of IGI records (about 36 million, or 41%). These English marriage, birth, and christening entries are especially useful for her pre-1837 (i.e., pre-vital registation) era. Scotland also has good representation, about 7.5%; the rest of the British Isles accounts for 3%. Other areas well represented are the Scandinavian countries, about 15%; central European countries (such as Austria, Germany and Switzerland), about 12%; North America (United States and Canada), also about 12%--with proportionally many more records for New England, than the Southern or Western States; and Mexico, about 7.5%.

South European, Latin American, African, and Asian countries are poorly represented at present. But because of the correlation between names appearing on the IGI and LDS temple work, and because LDS temples were recently completed in the latter three of these areas, you can expect to see better future IGI representation for many of these (especially Latin American and Far Eastern) countries.

As the IGI does not include living people, you generally won't need to check this source until you have extended your pedigree back to the 19th century (about 3-5 generations). The branch librarian will help you find the appropriate IGI microfiche for your country and surname. (You also need to know *state* for the USA, and *county* for England and the Scandinavian countries.) Within each locality, entries are arranged alphabetically (first by surname, then by given name) and thereafter chronologically (i.e., earliest entry of a name listed first). Wales and the Scandinavian countries, however, whose patronymic naming systems lend themselves better to alphabetical arrangement by given name, are so arranged.

Usually names of similar sound are interfiled, but check any cross-references given, and other spelling variations. Hyphenated surnames, or those with prefixes, such as *Mac*, *O'*, or *Van der*, may require extra care to find as they may have been entered differently, or part of the name dropped. (The name *O'Reilly*, for example, may also have been input as *Reilly*, *OReilly*, or *O Reilly*; each variant may possibly be found in separate locations.) Geographical boundary changes may also require that you search in more than one place. For instance, you may find a 1790 marriage or birth reported under West Virginia, even though that state wasn't formed from Virginia until 1863. Countries formerly part of the old German or Austro-Hungarian empires, due to frequent boundary changes, are often subject to like problems, so *check in each location within whose earlier or later borders an ancestor's vital events may have occurred.* (See Chapter 9.)

Once a desired entry is located, you may find information about your ancestor as extracted from a birth, christening, marriage, will, or census record. In some cases, though, the information may have been submitted by a relative of yours (perhaps distant, and unknown to you) as a member of the LDS Church. Record the batch and sheet numbers occupying the last two columns on the IGI microfiche, then look these up on an associated microfiche set to find the actual source of the data; don't hestitate to ask a branch librarian for assistance here. If the IGI information was extracted from a microfilmed parish register, the librarian can usually then assist you in ordering that microfilm.

It is a good idea to consult the original record indexed by the IGI, or any other secondary source, whenever possible. Sometimes mistakes were made, especially if the handwriting was difficult to read. Examination of the original record will identify such problems, as well as supplying possible additional facts not included on the IGI. Computer printouts are available for many of the towns and parishes whose vital records have been extracted by the GSU (in the USA, these are mostly for New England). Use the *Parish and Vital Records Lists* to learn if any exist for the towns or parishes you wish to research.

If the source of information was an LDS Church member, you may then order a photocopy of the original submission entry. This will include the submitter's name, and, often, relationship, as well as source of information used. Pay particular attention to this latter. If a secondary source was used, the resulting IGI data may not be as "good" as if extracted from a primary source (see Chapter 8). Nevertheless, learning of someone else who has previously conducted research on one of your lines can be valuable; contact this person, if possible. A set of instructions for the IGI called *IGI Instructions and Regions* is available in the branch libraries. A research paper for the 1984 edition of the IGI may also be purchased from the GSU. You will want to study these if you find much IGI ancestral information.

CATALOGS AND LOAN SYSTEM

The *Genealogical Library Catalog (GLC)* at one time was only available on microfilm. But over the past few years this information has gradually been automated and added to the computerized catalog database from which more recent COM copies of the GLC have been created. Each new COM edition of the GLC thus became more and more complete. In 1986 a part of the nearly-completed catalog was put onto *CD-ROM (Compact Digital--Read Only Memory) where it was available via computer terminals in the Main Library as a part of the GIS prototype recently tested there.

Testing showed that most library-users liked this newer format for the GLC. While searches were rather slow on the prototype (about 30 seconds each) revisions since then have quite reduced this retrieval time as well as otherwise improving it. No date has been announced for the first public CD-ROM release of the GLC; if all goes well, it may be during 1988. This first release will be capable of both locality and surname searching, and of printing out the resulting data screens. The second release will add census, film-number, author, and title searching capabilities; while the third will add subject and book call-number searching capabilities.

Full conversion from the paper (card) catalog to the electronic computer catalog will be finished sometime in 1987. Thus, the same complete GLC bibliographic data will appear in both of its next releases, i.e., as COM (in which form it will appear in most branch libraries) as well as on CD-ROM (in which form it will appear first at the Main library and, a little later, in selected branch libraries). The GLC consists of these parts:

(1) The alphabetical *Surname Catalog* indexes each main surname found in their collection of family history books acquired since 1978; so is well worth checking.

(2) The *Author-Title Catalog* and (3) *Topical Subject Catalog* allow you to find items using traditional author, title, and subject approaches.

(4) The *Locality Catalog* is especially helpful. It lists each record under the geographical place-name to which it pertains. (Thus, if a geographical name does not appear, that means the GSU presently has no records for that area.) The placenames are all alphabetically listed under their next-larger jurisdictions. So look up the state/country first; following that heading, check for the county/district of your interest. Lastly look following the county/district records for any city/town whose borders lie within it. The

sources themselves are grouped by subject following the place-name to which they pertain, and are also in alphabetical order. So *Census Records* preceed *Land Records*, preceed *Map Records*, preceed *Probate Records*, etc. (Appendix B, as it includes the subject headings used by the GSU, will be helpful here.)

(The *Locality Catalog* is not as complicated to use as this description may sound. And the CD-ROM version, as it will be accompanied by *how-to* menu screens, and will have incorporated the latest advances in design technology, is expected to be extraordinarily easy to search, even for a first-time user.)

After using the GLC to find needed items, a helpful loan system connecting the branch libraries with the main library, allows you to order those materials. Microfilm loan fees, to cover postage and handling, are $2.50 (for 2 weeks) or $3.00 (for 6 months) per roll. And photocopies can be made from their collection: $.15 per published book page, or $.25 per microfiche/microfilm page. There are no other costs involved in library use.

Some large branch libraries (e.g., in Santa Monica, California, or Idaho Falls, Idaho) keep a substantial permanent collection on the premises, so that you can use these microfilms without having to pay order fees. Even smaller branches often keep pertinent microfilms for nearby counties. The small one closest to us, for example, has microfilmed early records for several neighboring Virginia, West Virginia, North Carolina, and Tennessee counties.

FAMILY REGISTRY

A genealogical tool recently developed by the GSU is the *Family Registry*. Those willing to respond to other interested researchers are invited to submit their names, as well as as the names and data about those whom they are researching, onto forms at the branch libraries, or from:

Genealogical Department—Family Registry,
2nd Floor, West Wing
50 East North Temple Street
Salt Lake City, UT 84150

Your submission will be added to an updated COM index that is currently being issued quarterly, allowing those researching related lines to contact you. Prior to your own registration, look up the surnames of your interest on the alphabetical *Family Registry Index* to find related researchers. For any pertinent entries found, use the FR number to locate a copy of the original registration form on an allied microfiche set. The names, addresses, and, often, phone numbers of the registrants are given in both places.

Some 192,000 have registered their names in this collection since its inception in November, 1983. Some large non-LDS libraries, e.g., the Dallas and Los Angeles Public, National Genealogical and New England Historic Genealogical Societies, also have COM copies of this collection. A new version of the *Family Registry* is planned to be included within the GIS as it becomes more fully implemented, with those entries referenced to the appropriate pedigree and family group charts comprising the Ancestry File (see later).

GSU RESEARCH AIDS

Many research papers and other reference aids have been written by genealogical experts on the staff of the GSU. These constitute a good source of free and inexpensive help to both beginning and more advanced genealogists. They often supply the details you'll later need to make up and carry out an effective research plan. For example, they include *how-to's* for researching each of the United States; most countries of the world; certain ethnic groups; and various kinds of records. Some are so broad as to list dozens of pertinent records available for a particular country, what time periods and groups of people they cover, and where and how to obtain them. Others are very narrow; such as those giving addresses, and sample letters written in the native language, to request data from a foreign official.

Their *outlines* and *research aids* provide basic information, are quite brief, and aimed at the beginning researcher. These are presently being revised with the intention to have them stocked at the GSU and at its branch libraries where you may obtain a single copy of an individual item at no cost. You may also send an SASE (self-addressed, stamped envelope) to request a desired one of these from the GSU. Their *research papers* are more lengthy and detailed; even experienced genealogists should find them helpful. Their cost range is about $1.25 to $3.50, and they are sold by the Salt Lake Distribution Center. Contact a nearby LDS Church or branch genealogical library to find a price list for, and to order, these latter.

AIS INDEXES

In 1984 the GSU acquired COM copies of Accelerated Indexing Systems' *AIS Indexes* or *Searches*. These include 37 million names extracted from numerous American documents, especially early census indexes. Although providing fairly good coverage of a few colonial locations, its main value is in indexing the federal censuses of 1790 through 1850 (some 1860-1880 censuses are also included).

Unfortunately, the *AIS Indexes* contain errors. The most serious are generally errors of omission (i.e, not including on the index one who appeared on the census). And where actual census data is included, some of these numbers are wrong. A less serious error is including the same person two or more times. Still other errors, being typographical or transpositional, may not be serious enough to keep you from finding your ancestor using extra searching effort. For instance, names may be incorrectly listed as *Goerge* instead of *George*, *Lemmon* instead *Lennon*, or *Weeland/Wallen/Whellon* instead of *Whalen*, etc. Thus, *in using* a census, or *any* other *index, look for the desired name under all phonetic or other reasonable spelling variations*.

Because of their high error rate, don't consider the AIS Indexes fool-proof or complete. But as they do include so much of the population for so many successive decades, they must certainly be considered as one of the most comprehensive national sources yet assembled for this country, and their potential usefulness will be illustrated in later chapters. The *AIS Indexes*, by the way, aren't planned to be part of the GIS. And it should be noted that since they have been issued, other computerized census indexes have been issued that claim far better accuracy and completeness (for example, *Index Publishing*, mentioned in Chapter 12).

THE ANCESTRAL FILE AND PERSONAL ANCESTRAL FILE

The *Ancestral File* is a monumental source now being converted into a computerized database. This continues to be a massive project, with hundreds of volunteers spending thousands of hours entering several million pedigree and family group records at some two dozen sites throughout the country (as part of the earlier-described *name-extraction* program). These *Ancestral File* records have resulted mostly from a Church-wide submission program begun in the 1970's. But submissions are still being accepted from both members and non-members of this Church; request a free *how-to* brochure from the Ancestral File Unit of the GSU for details.

Some 15% of the *Ancestral File* records received to date were included and tested as part of the prototype GIS system during 1986. User response to the pilot project was, again, quite positive. So far, then, the *Ancestral File* appears to be making steady progress in reaching its objective: to compile huge amounts of family-submitted data into a format that is yet quick and easy to research. During 1987 the remainder of the entries making up this file will go into their powerful new mainframe computer for further search and retrieval testing. If successful, then, the Ancestral File will become fully operational as one of the first components of the GIS. As mentioned, this may occur as early as 1988. It will later be cross-referenced with entries similar to those found in the *Family Registry* (and perhaps other resource files).

Personal Ancestral File (PAF) is a genealogical software program developed by the GSU for home computer use. Specifics about this software are found in Chapter 4. That PAF and the Ancestral File share the same name is no coincidence. For PAF includes a utility known as *GEDCOM (see also in Chapter 4) for putting genealogical data into a standardized exchange format. And a main purpose for developing GEDCOM has been to make large-scale, rank-and-file input of family data into the *Ancestral File* (via personal computers) eventually possible. Currently, most of the pedigrees in this file extend back but four generations, but future submissions will go back much father. The database is thus planned to be an ever-growing and ever more valuable resource.

NEW AND DEVELOPING RESOURCES

While most 1987 efforts are concentrated on getting the *Ancestral File* up and running, there are still other resources being produced. One source just recently finished is *100 Most Used Books* (formerly projected to be *1,000 Most Used Books*; but copyright and other difficulties led to its downscaling). This valuable collection contains the full text of many of the most helpful genealogical references, and will be available as a COM collection at branch libraries in 1987.

Another large-scale computerized project now underway is name-extracting the complete 1880 USA census (mentioned further in Chapter 12). This project is expected to be finished in the early 1990's.

Even more exciting news is that the *name-extraction rate* is to be greatly increased over the next few years; being expected to reach 60 million yearly by early in the next decade. Many more online databases are expected to result and to be entered into the GIS from this effort. The GIS should thus become an incredibly large and valuable resource. More specific facts about these projects will be forthcoming. To learn of their completion in future years, stay in touch with a genealogical branch library. (We'll also include these details, as they become available, in our future editions.)

SUMMARY:

There are many helpful tools already available through the GSU and its associated branch libraries; and many more large and helpful resources in development!

(Note: *Asterisked terms are defined in the Technical Glossary found in Appendix G.)

Chapter 3. NOTE-KEEPING AND ORGANIZATION

Accuracy requires the sound organization of data that results from good note-taking and note-keeping skills; otherwise, a price will be paid later through unproductive hours spent in searching for facts that should be "right here," or in re-doing research improperly done the first time. Even more importantly, errors are sure to result from carelessness and poor organization that will negate the worth of your otherwise valuable research. Sound organization can also help point out the logical next steps to take in your research project.

Nevertheless, beginners commonly skip lightly over record-keeping. Any type of, or lack of, system, seems sufficient at first. It isn't until reaching a certain "critical mass" of data that a system's inadequacies, there from the beginning, suddenly become apparent. As may happen, for example, when Uncle George gives you his family scrap books full of facts collected over a 50 year period.

Beginners are typically surprised at the amount of data they soon accumulate. And large amounts of ancestral facts certainly may provide a good basis for certifying your family tree. Yet this is true only to the extent you can find a specific fact when needed. This means not only accurately recording your data, but also keeping efficient track of it.

In light of recent advances, there is no question but that computers do offer us the most potentially efficient means of data accuracy and control; yet, a computer applied to a messy system full of inaccuracies will simply speed up the mess and multiply the errors. Therefore, with or without such electronic aids (covered in the next chapter) you still must first understand and apply the basics of a soundly organized system, as we will now consider.

RECORD-KEEPING CRITERIA

What are the best record-keeping systems? Any of a number of methods will do, as long as the chosen system fulfills these three criteria:

o enables you to easily retrieve your materials after filing them;

o provides for meticulous documentation of all research information;

o is not overly-complicated or time-consuming to maintain.

Although criteria one and three are becoming much easier to fulfill with good computer software, yet faithful, conscientious observance of proper documenting procedures (explained in the "Recording and Documentation" section of Chapter 1) is always required, regardless of whether using high- or low-tech in your record-keeping system. The following section includes other essential observances. Asterisked suggestions apply mainly to manual systems, while non-asterisked apply to all:

RECORD-KEEPING SUGGESTIONS

* Keep notes on standard-size paper. Use notebook or legal size paper as preferred; however, it will simplify matters if the paper you use for note-keeping is the same size as your genealogical forms. The standard LDS charts that used to be legal sized have recently been revised so as to be notebook or letter-size (see in Appendix H). As this paper size is generally easiest to obtain, most people will prefer it for reasons of both convenience and economy.

*   Avoid coming to a library or courthouse so ill-prepared that you end up writing information on scraps, envelope backs, and checkbook stubs! Such odd-sized items seem mysteriously, but inevitably, to disappear.

*   Use only one side of a sheet of paper to record your notes. The reason for this will become apparent when you need to spread out your accumulated notes in front of you to find one particular piece of information. The more papers you have to examine, the more thankful you'll be not to have to flip each over and back again to find what you want.

*   Take your notes in pen where possible. Some libraries or archives, however, only allow the use of pencils. Then you had best use a fairly hard (#3) pencil to insure permanence.

o   Use only standard, if any, abbreviations so you will have no trouble in later interpreting them. In most cases, and especially for beginners, it's safer to record more than you think is needed to understand a given entry, rather than hurriedly abbreviating. This practice often leads to mistakes or leaving out something important. *And, obviously, illegibility or mistakes in handwritten notes must be avoided.

o   After you have gained enough experience to have a good feel for what is or isn't of genealogical value, you will want to use *abstracting*. This is the practice of taking out of documents only data of possible value. This can save much time, effort and frustration when working with long legal documents, such as land or probate records.

o   The best solution in most cases, and you'll usually find it more than worth the small expense involved, is to *photocopy* the desired record. (However, courthouses, archives, and other public record centers may charge, sometimes prohibitively, more for their photocopy services than libraries. So obtain that cost information in advance.) Remember to identify its source somewhere on the photocopy. If from a book or magazine, photocopy the title page and attach that as the bibliographic source. If from a courthouse, be sure to record location of the courthouse, room, binder, etc.

o   In all cases strive to be *excruciatingly meticulous*, a point that cannot be overemphasized. Reread your notes for accuracy at least once while the original is still in front of you. And a book reference, for instance, should include all bibliographic information (title, author, publisher, date of publication, library where found, and call number).

o   Be sure to note any record inadequacies. If, while searching the 1870 microfilmed census of Horry Co., SC, for example, you find many pages so faded as to be illegible, be sure to record that fact along with any data found. This will enable you, or a later researcher, to understand why certain expected families were not found. And for the same reason make note of any entry difficult to read or interpret.

*   Put each fact found about a family member, along with its source, onto every applicable family form. The deathdate for your grandfather, for instance, should be recorded on the family group charts where he appears as husband of your grandmother, as child of your great-grandparents, and on the appropriate pedigree chart. We have also found it helpful to record likely relatives (e.g., someone who often witnesses your ancestral records). While this will results in many more additional charts, yet many of these do turn out to be relatives, and having information on them may thus prove helpful. Here, of course, it may become difficult to keep track of many additional, possibly-related, families; in which case a computerized database may provide excellent assistance.

A SUGGESTED NOTE-FILING SYSTEM

This filing system is a slightly expanded version of one that has worked well for many people; it includes the following:

Family Folders: Keep your family notes and information in a regular, or legal-sized manila folder. You may begin by keeping all information on the Jones branch of your family in one folder. But when that folder starts getting fat, or it becomes time-consuming to locate information, you'll then want to divide up its contents so as to have a separate folder for each particular family of "Joneses" on which you have collected information.

Keep your *family folders* in alphabetical order according to surname, and than alphabetize within that surname by first name of the husband. This means his name is used as identification put onto the folder tab, along with birth and death dates and residence. That way, if you have several heads of families with identical names (four John Jones, for instance) you can arrange them chronologically with the youngest first: John JONES, Boston, MA 1827-1876, before John JONES, Boston, MA 1801-1837, before John JONES, Boston, MA 1778-18??. This makes it simple to locate any given family within your set of files.

If the family you're researching lived in more than one place, it may be helpful to have a separate folder for each of those locations. This is another way to divide the bulk when research notes start accumulating on a particular family.

Correspondence Log: Much valuable research can be accomplished through correspondence (see Chapter 15), and it helps to keep good records of this. One easy way is to attach a carbon or photocopy of your original letter to its reply. Give them both the same identifying number. #1 will be the first letter you send, #1A its reply, #2 the second letter you send, #2A its reply, etc. Keep them all attached to a *correspondence log*, illustrated in Figure 2. For each family you'll have one such file kept in that family's folder.

CORRESPONDENCE LOG: Cyrus BROWN, Mary FUNK			
#/DATE SENT	**NAME/ADDRESS**	**PURPOSE/REQUEST**	**ANSWER DATE**
1/8 Feb 83	D. Showalter 15 Rio St., Lime, CA	Obtain family charts	30 Aug 83
2/9 Aug 83	R. Showalter 3rd St., Rye, OH	Obtain family charts	17 Sep 83
3/9 Nov 83	Clerk Rocky Mt. KS	Brown/Funk Entries	3 Oct 83

Fig. 2. Example of a Correspondence Log

Document File: Documents are the important original records that allow you to learn and verify family information. These may be kept in the same family folder to which they apply, or within a separate file. Let's suppose, for example, you're successful when writing a courthouse to obtain a photocopy of an ancestor's will. After examining and recording the pertinent facts found within it onto the appropriate forms, you may want to place it for safe-keeping in a separate document file. This may also be arranged alphabetically by surname to ensure easy retrieval. Be sure to use cross-indexing anytime a source has information on more than one family. If your Brown document or folder, for instance, also has information pertaining to your Showalter and Funk families, then note that in your Showalter and Funk files.

Research Agenda: Your *research agenda* should play a helpful role in your notekeeping system. (In some genealogy texts, this is also referred to as a research "calendar" or "log.") It is simply a sheet of lined paper attached on top of your research notes. In the left-most column you describe the various *sources* which you intend to, or have already searched. (Later chapters will instruct you as to what specific sources you may list here.) An adjoining column will record the *purpose* of your search; another, *date* searched; and, lastly, the *results* of that search (for example, "nothing found," or, "see notes p. 5"). Keep this aganda current and it will be a convenient and useful index to your research.

```
┌─────────────────────────────────────────────────────────┐
│  RESEARCH AGENDA: Cyrus BROWN—Mary FUNK                  │
└─────────────────────────────────────────────────────────┘
```

SOURCE: What & Where	SEARCH PURPOSE	DATE	RESULTS
Brown Fam Bible; Diane Showalter, Solon, OH	Names/dates/places; vital statistics	9 Jul 83	Photocopy; doc. file
Land recs (DB#2) Probate recs(WB#1) Sassafrass Co. CH	Date to Kansas; whence; date of Cyrus' death	15 Oct 83	Photocopy; doc. file
1900, 1910 Box Co. CO censuses micro #456123	Birthdates/places: Mary/her parents/children; & marriage date to James	6 Nov 83	Extracts pp. 1-4
HARD ROCK VITAL RECS by J. Bigler (F477/B2) (Sass. Co. Library)	Any family data	3 Dec 83	Nil; wrong time period

```
┌─────────────────────────────────────────────────────────┐
│        Fig. 3. Example of a Research Agenda              │
└─────────────────────────────────────────────────────────┘
```

Summary Sheet: We lastly recommend your keeping a *summary sheet* current each time research is done. Your dated entries should include each detail discovered, as well as possible implications. Ask yourself questions such as, "What, if any, facts or clues have I obtained from this source?" "How does this fit with previously known facts?" and, "What further sources to research do these findings suggest?" Then write down the answers. The purpose of keeping such a written record, of course, is to ensure rigorous analysis each time research is conducted.   Such headwork is a necessary part of successful research any field.   Too many researchers are willing to spend hours examining records, but then don't discipline themselves to spend the additional minutes needed to analyze and write up their findings.   The result is waste.   Almost always, as the Chinese proverb aptly states: "the palest ink is better than the best memory."

Keeping your agenda and summary sheet up-to-date and your files in order not only helps your research progress in a logical and efficient manner; but provides additional benefits.   For instance, you will be able to come back to your notes even years later, if need be, and still be able to continue from where you left off without having to repeat previously done research. You can also sleep better knowing that if something happens to you, your research system is straight-forward and self-explanatory enough for another to continue, without having to repeat the valuable hours of research already accomplished.

Miscellaneous Files: A final suggestion to round out this note-keeping system should prove valuable: keep additional separate file folders for miscellaneous categories.   Have one, for instance, labelled, "research ideas" and write these down for inclusion here whenever they occur to you.   Also use it to list potentially helpful sources you may come across for a branch of the family not now being investigated.   Or when you obtain maps and gazetteer excerpts on an area you're researching, then it will be convenient to have them in a folder so labelled ("geography--early Massachusetts," for example).

WHAT TO INCLUDE IN YOUR NOTES

Although most of this chapter concerns the *hows* of notekeeping, here are also a few important reminders as to the crucial *whats* of notekeeping.

Persons to Research: The persons you will be interested in are *all* those with the same (or a variant of the) surname(s) you have chosen to research, in the place and time-period known to have been inhabited by your ancestral family.   It's best to take notes even on those who may be presently unknown to you for two reasons:

o   First, and most important, they may be in some way related.   Possibly they are members of the very family you're searching.   After all, if you already knew everything about them you wouldn't find it necessary to be conducting this search.   And even if more distantly related, facts about them may still be relevant to your family.

o   Second, it will help reduce possible confusion and misinterpretation of your research results if you can sort each person with the same surname into their member families, whether they are related or not.   Some records, such as the censuses beginning with 1850, may enable you to easily accomplish this.   And knowing, for instance, which Browns in Sassafras Co. belong to which family group may help you, through the process of elimination, to solve your research problems.

We will say, for example, you find that each head of the Brown families in Hard Rock, Kansas, in the last quarter of the nineteenth century, left wills naming their family members *except* the Cyrus Brown you are researching.   You are naturally disappointed, but if you have been diligent in collecting other Brown data in Hard Rock records, the names given in these wills may yet be of benefit; for you may now eliminate them as members of your Cyrus Brown's family. ·Remaining Browns, as found in other records, may therefore include members of his family. (See Chapter 14 for suggestions to prevent the mistaken identification errors often associated with a name so common as Brown.   Another good source is *Tracing Ancestors with Common Surnames* (Arlene H. Eakle, Author, 1984).

Information to Record: Suppose you find a reference to your Cyrus Brown in a land abstract record while conducting library research. This gives a date, and amount of acres purchased, in Hard Rock, Kansas. You are interested in a birthdate for your Cyrus, and therefore won't need to make note of this information, right? Wrong! Because our facts must often be deduced from circumstantial evidence, and because you can't expect to know in advance the importance of seemingly minor details in supplying that evidence, therefore, in taking notes, you need to include everything that *may* have a direct or indirect bearing on the problem. Especially as a beginner, don't expect to be a good judge of what later might be considered valuable. Prefer, therefore, to err on the side of taking *more*, rather than less, carefully-documented facts than you may think are needed.

SUMMARY

Here is a brief summary of how research notes, documents, and letters can be easily organized: keep one manila folder per family, identified on the folder-tab by the husband's name, life-span, and place of residence. In this folder you'll have a summary sheet and then at least two separate files:

o   *research notes*, kept together with an agenda on top, identifying each search you have done or intend to do.

o   *letters*, kept together with a correspondence calendar on top, also with their identifying numbers.

You may keep the *documents* for a family in their file; or you may alternatively put them together with those of other families in a separate, alphabetized, file. Additionally, make up *separate folders* for miscellaneous sources as needed.

Remember to take precise, detailed, documented notes of everybody with the surname(s) you're researching in every possibly helpful source. Thus committing yourself to accurately detail each family history search into a comprehensive, logical and organized system, naturally requires initial thought and diligence. Yet, we can promise you that by doing it right the first time around, the resulting efficiency will in the end save you much more time and energy than you'll expend. Additionally, such a system can help ensure the accuracy necessary to your future success. Those who have the opportunity to computerize their genealogical research should reap even noticeably greater benefits of organization and efficiency, if they choose wisely. How to do so will be covered next.

Chapter 4. COMPUTERIZATION

INTRODUCTION: Are you suited for computers; and are computers suited to you?

For most of us, it is only a matter of time before becoming inundated and overwhelmed by names, dates, notes, census records, ship lists, Aunt Maude's box of old letters, and other research materials we have collected. No wonder, then, as the personal computer (PC) becomes more affordable, productive, and easier to learn, that it is becoming an ever more popular component in our genealogy record-keeping systems. For potentially, at least, a PC does provide us the efficiency and speed to effectively store, organize, retrieve and exchange our research records.

Additionally, rapid technological progress increases both the scope and accessibility of the information we want. We have already seen that many computerized sources are now available to us whether we have a PC or not. But those of us with one may enjoy yet additional, growing research possibilities, such as rapid data exchange between our own PC, and other (including much larger) electronic systems.

On the other hand, an investment of your time and money is obviously needed to turn the potential advantages offered by a PC into actual help. And there are pitfalls awaiting the unwary. Fortunately, you need not fall into these. We trust this chapter will provide a safe foundation upon which you can confidently grow into a well-informed, competent computer-genealogist. If, indeed, that is what you want.

For we suggest you begin by simply thinking through some obvious questions: First, "Am I suited for computers?" (i.e., are you willing to invest time up-front for expected long-range results?) Not everybody is. In fact, from our experience, many who would greatly benefit from PC use are unwilling to pay the price of self-study and experimentation necessary to enjoy fully these blessings. In effect, they progress no further than the early "hold-my-hand" stage of learning.

In considering this question, it may help to recall how many of us successfully paid the price (feeling foolish and making dumb mistakes) to progress past the initial "kill-the-motor" stage of learning to drive a car. Obviously, as in any obtaining any new skill, the most important ingredient is the desire to learn, coupled with an investment of time and effort.

We thus suggest devoting about 10% of your time for about six months to learn about computers in general, and using your own PC system in particular. This is a lot, but by no means wasted, time. You will quickly progress to the point where not everything the computer does surprises you. And from then on you can expect to not only save time, but to enjoy the learning process. This, of course, is assuming you obtain a system adequate for your needs; which brings us to the second question of concern:

"Just what are my goals and how do I want my system to help me?" As mentioned before, simply applying the power of a PC to an otherwise messy system only speeds up the mess. On the other hand, by spending quality thought and serious study on your research, you will progress even without a PC, and more so with one.

> **Simply applying the power of a computer to an otherwise messy system only speeds up the mess.**

The last question is, <u>Are computers suited for me</u>? In other words, are there reasonably-priced and straight-forward systems to help accomplish your goals? Probably. But to find this out requires some understanding of the PC and its current status. Such background is what constitutes the remainder of this chapter. (Computer terms that may be new to you are marked with an asterisk and defined in the Appendix G—Glossary.)

NEEDED BACKGROUND

As a wise car-purchaser, you would first think through your wants, read current reviews, and ask friends about the models they like. You may even need to learn new terms (*rack-and-pinion steering*, or *strut suspension*). Lastly, you would search out a reliable dealer to test drive your top choices. A similar procedure is recommended for a PC. Decide what you want, then seek to gain the necessary background. This will include reading appropriate literature, talking with more experienced friends, and learning vocabulary. Lastly, you will find a reputable dealer to try out your top choices (an important strategy to avoid the consumer hassles possible with ANY purchase.) Gaining background need not be overly difficult; consider these points:

o Computers are becoming more and more *user-friendly*, i.e., easier to understand and operate without technical background.

o Learning how to use a PC effectively is, as mentioned, probably no more difficult (and certainly safer!) than learning to drive a car. You need not repair or program them.

o Local computer dealers should show you how to get started before purchase.

o There are numerous individuals and/or interest groups from whom you can receive help and answers to your questions.

o The manuals and handbooks that accompany PC products are improving; some are very good. (Many are still atrocious, however. You will want to check this out before purchase.) Our glossary (Appendix G) will help you with terminology. And there is a good general reference PC book (see later).

o Most good systems offer technical support over phonelines (several are even toll-free numbers!).

> **Learning how to use a PC effectively is probably no more difficult (and certainly safer!) than learning to drive a car.**

HOW COMPUTERS WORK

Your system will work similar to an office with files, cabinets, typewriter, and efficient secretary. The secretary's brain and organizing ability is represented by the operating system which enables the PC to run programs, work the printer, display information on the screen, and take into its memory information typed onto its keys. Each of your data *diskettes represents a drawer in a filing cabinet where different, uniquely-named, files are stored. The *disk drive is a slot in the PC where you insert the diskettes, allowing you to create or manipulate files using the PC's memory and abilities. Have your PC dealer show you the several steps involved in the actual use of a PC. (No need to deal with an uncooperative firm, by the way, as you are now in a buyers' market.)

A BASIC COMPUTER SYSTEM, and GENERAL BUYING RECOMMENDATIONS

Based on 1987 options, we would recommend the following hardware (equipment) and other PC system components:

o a *computer* with a keyboard that feels comfortable, *function keys, at least one serial and one parallel *port, and lots of memory (see section to follow)

o a *monitor* or screen displaying 80 characters side to side and 24 lines from top to bottom.

o two double-sided *disk drives*, OR, even better for not much more cost, a *hard disk* in combination with one or two disk drives. Again, this will multiply storage capacity.

o numerous blank *diskettes*.

o an operating system. This necessary low-level software allows your PC to work with other parts of your system, such as printers, monitors, and compatible software. We generally recommend version 2.1 or greater of *PC-DOS or *MS-DOS (i.e., to run an IBM, or compatible) as there is presently more software useful to the genealogist which runs on that system, and so much less chance of compatibility[1] problems.

o a *printer*. Compatibility comes into play here as well. Printers normally come ready to be connected to either the PC's parallel or serial *port. (The former requires only that you attach one end of the connecting cable to the printer and the other to the PC's parallel port. Serial printers, however, can be quite a hassle to set up; not all serial connectors are compatible.) Three of the most common types of printers are: *daisy-wheel; *dot-matrix and *laser. We recommend a top-quality dot-matrix. Currently their versatility surpasses, and quality rivals, that of either of the others; yet they are less expensive to operate. (The entire text of this book was produced on a NEC P6 dot-matrix printer we bought for under $500, using a typesetting program, LePrint, v. 2.)

o last, and most important, *software programs*.

HARDWARE ADVANCES in MEMORY and STORAGE

Processing much data requires much memory. And, until recently, large memory capacity has been expensive. Yet, because hardware has advanced so much in recent years (comparatively far more than has software) you need no longer skimp on memory or storage. A brief look at recent advances bears this out:

Barely 5 years ago, 64*K of *RAM (working memory to hold the equivalent of 32 typed, double-spaced pages) was heralded as a revolutionary new PC standard. And a couple years ago a 10MB hard disk (i.e. to store 10 million characters) was well over $1,000. Yet today, you can obtain an *XT-clone[2] providing ten times that working memory (i.e., 640K RAM) *with* a 20 *MB hard disk for under $1,000, the XT being considered now a low-end system!

---

[1] Notwithstanding PC benefits, millions have been wasted on unwise purchases. And underused, soon-obsolesced machines result mostly from incompatibility. Stay in the mainstream, then, to ensure that the best programs will run on your machine.

[2] Economical IBM *clones* to this point have provided us some good to excellent buys. But models do vary in compatibility, (so try out your software in advance to make sure it runs). And unfortunately, some clone companies may "go under" due to the more powerful and difficult-to-clone IBM models introduced in April, 1987.

The more powerful *AT (*Advanced Technology* or '286) introduced in 1984; and even more, the recently-introduced, powerful *'386 system, have the potential to remove memory constraints altogether (using an improved *operating system, OS/2, that should become available in early 1988).

And, in addition to the undisputed storage favorites: hard disks and floppy diskettes, optical disks now offer us a promising alternative by storing many hundred *MB on small, removable disks or cartridges. A CD-ROM stores as much as 550 (360K) floppies, and a *Worm* (writeonce, read many times) optical disk cartridge stores almost that much. IBM has recently introduced a relatively-economical *Worm* optical disk drive. So we can now look forward to this former *niche* technology becoming mainstream technology.

Almost without noticing it, then, we appear to not only have reached, but to have already far surpassed, a long-cherished dream; i.e., being able to economically computerize and store all the known relatives we may individually care to. Yet we may not stay satisfied for long, as we note the far more interesting vistas now opening ahead. And given these emerging high-end possibilities, who can blame us for entertaining yet higher-end dreams: Why not combine these, our individual databases, to create significantly larger and more helpful (community, state, and eventually national) databases? Electronic means now exist to compile, store and search potentially huge databases. Then why not cooperatively share the data that *en masse* can provide solutions to our joint research challenges? Indeed, a number of forward-looking genealogists are now beginning to do just that.

We can be making steady, if initially slow, progress in reaching such lofty goals even while, as in our case, still using an "outdated" XT-Clone. Besides being relatively inexpensive, an XT runs most of today's genealogically-helpful software, and, with a large capacity hard-disk, is fast. We like ours enough, in fact, that we're now planning to build another. But we'll add an even higher-capacity disk to help us pursue a particular dream of ours: cooperatively compiling a genealogical database for early Virginia.

In deciding on your system size, consider following a similar approach. That is, using the *price-to-power* ratio, as well as your actual and projected needs for the next little while, look for the maximum memory and storage *for the money* in an IBM-compatible[1] system. In almost every case a best buy will lie about midway between the newest ultra-powerful technology; and incompatible, low-powered, un-upgradable systems. And if you, like us, expect extra-large storage needs, you can gratefully look forward to these inevitabilities: 1) prices will fall for the more powerful hardware systems; and 2) software will be developed to tap the power of the newer hardware.

BENEFITS of COMPUTERIZATION

With sufficient memory, storage capacity, and good software; you can efficiently handle a growing volume of data, and still enjoy the greatest benefits of computerization: *speed*, so you can search instantaneously through thousands of names to find the few fulfilling a certain requirement; *accuracy*, so the exact facts found in your raw data are those printed out on your forms; *reproducability*, so you can use the same facts over and over after entering them only once; and *sortability*, so you can re-arrange and list records in any desired way, such as chronologically, or into an alphabetized name index, for instance. Here are other abilities you'll want to consider:

o <u>Writing and typesetting</u> are greatly simplified through *word processing software to make for easy publication of your documented and researched family histories. Several good genealogical programs can output your data into a camera-ready, indexed book. *Roots II* (see later) even provides automatic pagination of both book and index.

And it's not hard to turn unorganized genealogy notes into ordered files using the search feature found in a good word processor program. Just type all your notes into large files. Then use the search ability to quickly locate and put into separate, newly-created, files all notes pertaining to each desired family or surname. Within these new files, you can now easily organize and analyze your work. From that point, or if just starting, use your word processor to keep research agendas and summary sheets updated (see Chapter 3).

o Advanced software, such as full-text retrieval (e.g., *ZyIndex*) and free-form text-oriented database programs (e.g, *askSAM*) provides superior organizational and retrieval abilities. Thus, you can compare your families for any given variable (name, date, or location); or assemble them into contemporary neighborhood, multi-generational family, or any other group you want to examine. This could be most useful for studies larger than could be handled by a regular genealogy software program.

o Laptop P.C.'s allow for directly typing in your research and bibliographic notes Newer laptops are quite powerful, but are also, compared to a desktop, quite high-priced. You may again prefer an "out-dated" (i.e., older, less-powerful, but economical) model.

o Optical scanning systems may soon provide us even more time-savings. Image scanners produce the equivalent of "digital microfilm" by storing text or data graphically into a computer. A companion technology is optical character recognition (OCR), in which words are recognized and converted into *ASCII code, so as to be manipulatable by a word processor. The two technologies, now beginning to merge, are progressing rapidly. An example of the current state-of-the-art is a Canon laser scanner with OCR software, retailing for $1,800, that inputs both type- and computer print (mono- and proportionally-spaced) into a PC at 12 seconds per page. (More expensive models can do this with typeset books.) And, as OCR software continues to improve, it may even allow the powerful '386 machine to itself be used as a scanner. We thus optimistically anticipate the eventual demise of that ever-tedious chores: manual note-taking. (Potentially more helpful is equipment being developed to electronically decipher handwriting. But don't look for these anytime soon!)

o Several good genealogical programs include the helpful *soundex feature allowing you to search out most name variants within your database.

o Telecommunications is the area where many of us expect the most exciting future developments in computer-genealogy to lie. Fast research of online databases within your own home, and use of genealogical bulletin boards, are already popular.

SOFTWARE, INCLUDING CURRENT GENEALOGY SOFTWARE

Software, or the programs used to run a PC, are the most essential elements in your system. Many powerful, easy-to-operate programs exist. Yet it is also true that software abilities (indeed, whether or not you can even use it!) greatly depends on the *hardware, or computer, upon which it runs. So, before buying your PC, it's wise to make sure it runs the programs you want to use. Also, as a rule of thumb (to avoid likely *bugs) don't purchase a first version of any hardware or software.

Choosing software is a challenge. Therefore read as many reviews, and try out as many good programs as possible. A good source of general advice is: *The Whole Earth Software Catalog* (1985; $17.50; Doubleday Publisher). It's kept current through updates found in the quarterly magazine, *Whole Earth Review*, and in online systems such as *CompuServe* (GO WEC at any prompt) and EIES (Public Conference 1031). We especially like its *SHOPPING* section (*Strategies, Criteria of Software Excellence*, etc.). Read this early in your computer career, and you may save yourself from expensive mistakes, as well as untold frustration.

We admit a bias towards speed, power, control, and ease of operation, and so may be less tolerant than you of slow, cumbersome or overly-difficult-to-learn programs. But you may nevertheless still want to consider following our example. That is, be a software skeptic. Approach your software decision the same way that a confirmed bachelor would approach a potential marriage partner. Certainly not just anybody, nor just any software, will do.

> **We believe this is the best criterion for knowing when you have found software that adequately meets your needs: you will have fun using it.**

There are several hundred genealogical programs now available; their quality varying widely. Most are amateurishly written and not worth your serious investigation. But there are a few good ones. We have selected from those programs with MS-DOS versions (this being by far the most popular operating system for the new generation of genealogy programs) those we believe are now the best, and are most likely to keep improving (i.e., the software developers continue to actively revise and improve their product). And see order-form at end of book to obtain more extensive reviews.

o Dollarhide's *Family Research Manager (FRM)* introduced in 1986 costs $195. We rate it good. We expect, however, those with computer experience may lose patience, as we did, with its word processor; we found it simply too time-consuming to learn, given the many other excellent, and much easier-to-learn word processors. But we did like how it handled the important job of genealogical documentation. (See later for free demo disk details).

o Quinsept's *Family Roots (FR)* is $185. It has long provided good user support, and many hardware versions, to make it a deservedly popular program. We didn't have the chance to review yet the new Version 3.0, but will soon. We understand extensive updating puts it in competition with *Roots II* as the current *top-of-the-line* genealogical software. Several Apple (including Apple Pro Dos 3.4 and Apple Dos 3.3) and an MS-DOS version are now ready, while a Macintosh[3] version is being released incrementally (editing and chart-making installments are out as we go to press). The Commodore 64 (because of hardware limitations, a much less powerful) version is scheduled for a later update; but their TRS-80 and other, older CP/M versions are not. (A demo disk-tutorial manual package is $9.95 from Quinsept, Inc., Box 216, Lexington, MA 022173.)

o *My Roots* by Mark Peters is another program we plan to review. It supposedly offers good genealogical documentation features for MS-DOS and Apple II machines. Version 3, done in 1986, retails for $99.95.

o *Personal Ancestral File (PAF)* version 2.0, was developed by the GSU, and is already a popular choice for owners of MS-DOS, Apple II, and *CP/M (in the Kaypro format) machines. A Macintosh[3] version will be out by late 1987. Order from the LDS Church Distribution Center, 1999 West, 1700 South, Salt Lake City, UT 84140; or obtain more details by writing the GSU, c/o *Ancestral File Operations Unit*. We found it an excellent value for only $35. While slower than we like on data input, our biggest disappointment was that you can't integrate its excellent "Research Data Filer" with its own "Family Records" program. So it can't yet be used to write a computerized, indexed family history (as is possible with *Roots II, FRM, Family Roots* or *My Roots*).

---

[3] The Mac II is a powerful machine, optionally IBM-compatible, but still quite expensive as we go to press. While the older Macintosh does not have the IBM option, genealogical software written just for it is finally becoming available.

o *Patriarch* (for Apple IIs) by J.D. Gerhan was developed specifically for handling Jewish genealogy, whose record-keeping requirements differ fundamentally from Anglo-Saxon methods. It is, for example, descendent-oriented, in contrast to the pedigree chart format which is ascendent. It also provides for numerous user-defined fields. Those researching ethnic groups requiring a great amount of flexibility (or who may otherwise just enjoy having that option) may want to investigate this program. (We have not.) It costs $95.

o *Roots II*, version 2, by *Commsoft* costs $195. It's a fast, sophisticated MS-DOS database program. It can even run (although more slowly) on an older IBM-PC with only 64K. We enjoyed learning and using it more than any genealogical program we have as yet tried, and would have to rate it as "one of," if not THE *top-of-the-line* in today's genealogical software. We warn you that it will probably take awhile to learn how to become proficient with its many good features as the manual is not as well-written as the program. But you will probably consider the time well-invested, considering the effective results it makes possible. It even has the ability to graphically store maps and photos.

Roots II needs to be used in conjunction with a word processor to make up the genealogical documentation files supporting your entered data. Using *function and other keys, it is simple to go back and forth between its database and your other programs. We advise your doing this whenever necessary to document each of your sources. *The program otherwise provides but very brief, and thus generally inadequate, documentation files.* The second version is no longer *copy-protected. (Many of us dislike copy protection as it increases operational difficulties and, more importantly, the possibility of serious data loss.)

Lastly, a couple important software reminders: First, be sure to register it by returning the manufacturer's card that accompanies it. That way, the software developer will keep you informed of updates and other program improvements. Second, while using your software, remember Murphy's Law and *make back-ups* each time you add to or change anything of importance in your database. We further recommend keeping your back-up copies separate, just in case data in one of these locations is accidently lost or destroyed.

NON-GENEALOGY SOFTWARE & INDUSTRY STANDARDS (ASCII & GEDCOM)

You may not want to limit your investigation to specialized genealogical software. Many professional genealogists (including ourselves) at this point still prefer and use non-genealogical software. At least partly this is because we deal with larger databases than the average family historian; partly it is because we think some of the non-genealogical (i.e., regular business or shareware) software is sometimes better for what it does.

Word-processing, filing, information retrieval and/or database management software all have their uses in genealogy. If already skilled in using one of these, you likely can judge its abilities to record, store, and search your data. Using a program you really like already, and that adequately fills your genealogical needs, will save you both learning-time and money.

An advantage enjoyed by many of the commercial or public domain software packages is their ability to produce standard *ASCII files. These are files that can be read by humans, as well as by most other computer programs so as to promote compatibility. The ability to produce ASCII files has been slow to come to genealogy software, but several recent program versions now provide this advantage; i.e., *Family Roots, My Roots, PAF*, and *Roots II*. ASCII is also the basis of *GEDCOM (GEnealogical Data COMmunications) being developed by the GSU as a standardized format to exchange genealogical data. GEDCOM thus takes compatability even one more helpful step further than ASCII by itself.

Like much that is helpful in computers, the technical make-up of GEDCOM is somewhat complex. Yet its purpose is simple: to transpose virtually any type or amount of genealogical data accurately and easily between any number of differing systems. While its structure need not be fully understood to be used successfully, yet the ideas behind it are again rather simple. Just as in an outline, where different numbers and letters are used to represent the levels and relationships of ideas, GEDCOM uses numbers and symbols to represent the levels and relationships of the names, dates, places, and other facts found within a genealogical database. Because GEDCOM is still being developed, however, it may be some years down the road before we fully realize all its benefits.

GEDCOM will do more than just allow us to enter data into the Ancestral File. By providing us a standard input/output format, it will overcome many present incompatability problems, and so advance the whole field.

SHAREWARE; A FREE SOFTWARE LEARNING TOOL

In your investigation of software, remember that while much of the good (and not-so good!) commercially-produced software is expensive, there are reasonably-priced, and even free, alternatives; viz., *public-domain* (i.e., non-copyrighted) and *user supported* software. The latter is known variously; e.g., *freeware*, *shareware*, or *teaseware* (this last being a limited, rather than a full version of a program).

Unlike the heavily advertised, often expensive, and sometimes copy-protected, commercially-available programs, the developers of user-supported software encourage sharing it. So obtain it free from a user-group or friend who already has it. If you you like it enough for sustained use, you are asked to register with the program author who, in turn, provides added support and updates. (These *registration* costs are usually quite reasonable in comparison to commercial prices.)

Such programs thus provide you a valuable but free *hands–on* opportunity to become experienced in computer use, and learn the features you like. (But you will still be spending valuable time, so even here you'll probably want to discriminate in favor of the more highly-recommended of these programs.)

PC user-groups have been the traditional place to learn about these (consult the group's *Software librarian* for details). And because so many of these are also available *online, local user-group bulletin boards, as well as some popular subscriber information services are also good sources. The two largest of the latter are *The Source* (which has a host of Apple and Macintosh programs) and *CompuServe*, whose free software is in their Special Interest Group Databases under *Data Libraries*).

Many private companies also specialize in offering public-domain software; some are listed below. Most charge a membership fee and a few dollars for a disk you could otherwise obtain free; yet they also often provide software descriptions and/or reviews through their publications and maybe technical service as well. We list here also guides that detail many thousand of these programs. (Note, though, that book listing become outdated quickly; catalogs revised at least annually may be more helpful):

o Glossbrenner, Alfred. *How to Get Free Software: The Master Guide to Free Programs for Every Brand of Personal or home Computer*. NY: St. Martin's Press, 1984. ($14.95).

o *Directory of Public Domain and User Supported Software*, 1986. $8.95 + $4 P&H; order from PC-SIG, 1030 E. Duane, Sunnyvale, CA 94086; 408-730-9291. (Glossbrenner says there are so many good programs in this catalog, "you'll think you've died and gone to free software heaven").

o *National Software Lending Library*: 507 Race St, Cambridge, MD 21613; 301-221-0051. 10,000 public domain programs (and still growing) for Apple, Atari, Commodore 64, IBM, Texas Instruments, Vic, and TRS-80's. Borrowing is free, but requires a $75/year membership; non-members may rent or buy.

o *The Apple Avocation Alliance*: 1803 Warren Ave., Cheyenne, WY 82001, 307-632-8561, is a commercial mail-order firm. $2 catalog lists over 350 public domain programs.

o *The Big Red Apple Club (BRAC)*: 1105 So. 13th St, #103, Norfolk, NE 68701, 402-370-4680; good; a monthly catalog with listings and descriptions of their disk offerings.

o *The Public Domain Exchange*: 2074C Walsh Ave, Santa Clara, CA 95050 (800-331-8125 for credit card orders outside of CA). *The Best of Apple Public Domain Software* (for Apple IIs; $6.95), and *The Best Mac Deal* ($7.95; both 150 pages), plus a quarterly bulletin and technical support for the Apple, Macintosh and IBM shareware they sell.

o *Shareware Express*: 31877 Del Obispo, Suite 102, San Juan Capistrano, CA 92675; $2 for a catalog with descriptions of all their user-supported and public domain programs.

o *U.S. Computer Supply*: 511-104 Encinitas Blvd, Encinitas, CA 92024; (800-992-1992 to request free catalog); thousands of public domain programs for IBM, Commodore, Apple, and CP/M machines.

o *The Boston Computer Society* (See later) offers a 100 page catalog of public-doman software; $10 for nonmembers, $7 for members.

o Froehlick Robert A. *The Free Software Catalog and Directory: the What, Where, Why, and How of Selecting, Locating, Acquiring, and Using Free Software.* NY: Crown Pub. Inc. 1984; (475 p., $9.95; mainly for C/PM systems); and *The IBM PC (& Compatibles) Free Software Catalog and Directory*. Dilithium Press, 1986; (984 p., $17.95).

> **"Shareware" and public-domain programs provide us a free chance to gain experience and discover which features we like.**

User-supported *Genealogy on Display*, for example, is written in Basic for MS-DOS machines. Version 5 can be obtained free off of genealogical bulletin boards, or by sending a blank *DSDD 5-1/4 inch diskette and self-addressed return mailer to Melvin O. Duke, POB 20836, San Jose, CA 95160. (A $35-45 contribution requested if you use and enjoy it). *Tracer* (compatible with, and faster than, PAF version 1) and *Family Ties* (for MS-DOS and CP/M) (the latter is also developing a non-shareware Macintosh 512 version) are two other shareware genealogy programs. While each is $50 to register, you can freely *download them from various BB systems.

The Dollarhide FRM demo disk is also considered a limited public domain software package; he encourages making copies to share with others. Send, as above, a *DSDD blank diskette and mailer to Dollarhide Systems, POB 3110, Blaine, WA 98230. A double disk, 256K minimum MS-DOS system is required (and write him if interested to learn about future Macintosh and Apple II versions).

We highly recommend, by the way, one of the more popular MS-DOS shareware programs, *PC-Write*. We have used it as our text editor for the past three editions of this book. It is a versatile, powerful program with many features found in expensive programs. Obtain free from a users group, or send $16 directly to Quicksoft (219 First N. #224, Seattle, WA 98109). (192K minimum recommended.) Optional registration ($89) for support and updates.

While the programs thus far named exemplify some of those you will want to investigate, yet by the time you read this, because of how quickly the field progresses, there may well be updated versions of these, or even completely new possibilities to consider, so you will need to obtain current facts. We suggest the following steps to do this: First (most important for those new to computers), contact the local user-groups for their help and suggestions. Second, browse the most recent issues of available PC magazines and the computer-genealogy periodicals listed below. Third, study the latest ads; paying more attention, of course, to specific features named, than to glossy ad lay-out, or general claims of superiority. (And keep in mind that user-supported software does little to no advertising; usually you learn about these through informed user-group members.) Fourth, fill out the order-form at the book's end to learn of future editions and Updates.

COMPUTER–GENEALOGY PERIODICALS and RELATED BOOKS:

o *The NGS CIG Digest*, Richard Pence, editor. Published bimonthly by the National Genealogical Society Computer Interest Group (see later); $5/year membership.

o *Genealogical Computing*, Paul Andereck editor, published by Ancestry, Inc., PO Box 476 Salt Lake City, UT 84110. $25/year; Quarterly.

o Andereck, Paul A. *Genealogical Computing: the Beginning*. Salt Lake City, UT: Ancestry Inc., PO Box 476 Salt Lake City, UT 84110, 1984. $25. (Digest of the early newsletters, so of historical interest)

o Andereck, Paul and Pence, Richard A. *Computer Genealogy: a Guide to Research through High Technology*. Salt Lake City, UT: Ancestry, Inc., 1985. $12.95 (for those experienced in genealogy).

o *The Genealogical Computer Pioneer* by Posey Enterprises, PO Box 338, Orem, UT 84057. $25/year; bi-monthly. (Updates and adds to reviews found in their book:)

o Posey, Joanna W. *Tracing Your Roots by Computer: The Applications Handbook*. Orem, UT: Posey International, Rev. 1986. $39.95. Software reviews covering all systems.

o Posey, Joanna W. *The Next Step* Orem, UT: Posey International, 1986. $29.95; preparing, printing, and marketing a computerized genealogy.

o *Computers in Genealogy*. Quarterly published by the Society of Genealogists, London, England. (Use of very low-cost PCs, programming in Basic, and use of generic programs stressed here and in book written by this periodical's former editor:)

o Hawgood, David. *Computers for Family History: an Introduction*. 1985. $5.00; order from 26 Clister Rd, London, W3 ODE, England.

You will have no trouble, of course, in locating general PC magazines (and the *Whole Earth Catalog* has a section rating these) but you may have trouble initially in understanding the articles. For, just as in the field of genealogy, a new vocabulary is also necessary to understand the world of computers. Many of these terms are defined in this chapter and in Appendix G. However, as in most aspects of this field, you'll progress fastest by talking with those who already have the background you seek. This brings us to a most important topic:

USER AND INTEREST GROUPS FOR HELP and SUPPORT

Support is the necessary knowledge, help, and encouragement you'll depend on so much at first. This can be supplied by a friend, relative, or PC dealer. Most often, however, it comes from fellow members of a PC user- or interest-group. Group memberships typically cost between $15 and $25/year and can be invaluable. So if you learn, for example, there is an excellent Apple user-group in your area and no other comparably good local support, then you may well be justified in changing your concern from, "which IBM-compatible software/hardware shall I get?" to "which Apple products will best suit my needs?"

Some benefits commonly offered by a PC user-group (look for these in your investigation) are: PC classes offered at no charge; substantial equipment (including blank diskette) discounts; newletters supplying updates as to what is happening in the rapidly-changing computer world; club libraries with hundreds of borrowable books and software; and member rosters so you know who to contact about what (and some do include a genealogy group roster).

> **Knowledge, help and encouragement can be supplied by a friend, relative or PC dealer; but most often comes from fellow user group members.**

The *Boston Computer Society (BCS)* is the largest (23,000 members at its recent one decade anniversary) and has been one of the best. It has 46 special interest groups (SIGs) covering virtually every hardware, and type of software, as well as diverse other topics (e.g., Artificial Intelligence, *CD-ROM, graphics, telecommunications, desktop publishing). Each SIG maintains free software collections. (Memberships, $35 regular; $24 youth/senior citizens; One Center Plaza, Boston, MA 02108; 617-367-8080.)

Most user-groups were created to help with a particular kind of hardware or software. Local PC user-groups are especially common in metropolitan and/or university centers. *Genealogical Computing* gives updated listings of computer-genealogy interest groups; many of these are set up on the state level. Here are some on the national level:

C-PAF-UG (Capitol PAF Users' Group)
POB 177
Bowie, MD 20715
New; $15/year, includes newsletter; monthly meetings and a bulletin board system.

KUGIG (Kaypro Users Genealogical Interest Group) c/o Alice Petersen
PO Box 1790
Ames, IA 50010
A commercial venture supplying genealogical templates/application programs for Kaypro, CP/M (& now DOS) PC's. And write if interested in a possible *FRM* users-group.)

NGS CIG (National Genealogical Society Computer Interest Group)
4527 17th St North
Arlington, VA 22207-2363 (See next page.)

QUG (Quinsept User-Group) c/o Bob Mitchell
102 Broadfield Ln
Spotsylvania, VA 22553-9101
Largest user-group; about 1700 USA members; helpful newsletter and online bulletin board (617-641-1080), now a part of the National Genealogical Conference (see later).

The *NGS CIG* recently instituted the National Projects Registry (NPR) database in which are described ongoing genealogical, non-family projects (including non-computerized). Registration onto this database is encouraged to reduce duplication, and increase cooperative efforts. (Request NPR registration forms from their Arlington address.) It also keeps members updated on current developments via a good bi-monthly newletter (see earlier); sponsors educational computer seminars, including those given at the yearly *National Genealogical Society* Conference; and also sponsers a node on the *National Genealogical Conference (NGC*, see next). Membership dues are only $5.00/year. (They will also encourage, but don't require, you to enroll in their excellent sponsering organization, the *National Genealogical Society*, with dues of $30/year.)

TELECOMMUNICATIONS AND MODEMS

A modem is a device allowing two or more computers to electronically communicate with each other over telecommunication lines (usually telephone lines). The speed at which information is exchanged is refered to as a baud rate. The higher the baud rate, the faster the transmission. Modems which can handle higher speeds are more expensive to buy, but more economical to use because the telephone connect costs are less. Currently, most PC databases and bulletin boards operate at 1200 baud; however, the use of 2400 baud will soon be widespread. We would suggest the purchase of a modem that can handle 2400 baud (these can also handle the slower 1200 rate), and communications software that can handle up to 9600 baud. Much of the best software with these capabilites, being "shareware," is not expensive. (For example, highly-rated *ProComm*, and our current choice, *Q-Modem*.)

Some telecommunication developments are potentially quite helpful in genealogical research. Online searching is one that will be detailed later. Searching the historical databases just recently available via "Knowledge Index" (see Chapter 6) may be of particular interest.

Another helpful possibility afforded by telecommunications is data exchange through online bulletin boards and electronic mail. While several genealogical bulletin boards have been started in the past, they have received little use (few genealogists then having modems) and consequently many "went under." This past year, however, two rather large national networks have begun, and so far are attracting many users. Each offers the attractive feature of low-cost dial-up rates for many areas.

One is a commercial venture sponsored by the *GE Network for Information Exchange (GEnie)*. GEnie is new, but already has become the third largest subscriber information center in the nation. Registration is $18/year; the cost is $5-7/hour for non-prime rate time using 300 or 1200 baud; and with local phone rates in over 550 American cities (call 800-638-9636 to learn which cities are included, or for more information.)

The *National Genealogical Conference (NGC)* began in May, 1986. It's free to use; simply register with one of the local *nodes, or through Confererence Coordinator, Ken Whitaker of *CommSoft* at 415-967-1900. Of course, only those residing in one of the local node areas would enjoy free modem-phone use as well. (About 20 nodes are presently joined; several in California, and one or more in Colorado, Delaware, Florida, Maryland, Massachusetts, New York, Ohio, Texas, Utah, and Virginia.)

NGC is a part of *Fidonet*, an international network of some 1,200 *nodes using *FIDO*, a shareware *bulletin board (BB) program, and its *Echomail* capabilities. Using the latter, any message entered in the "Genealogy Message Area" of any of the BBs is relayed on to all the others overnight. (And Mr. Magree, of *GEnie*, uploads messages of interest from the *NGC* onto his network as well.) Some of the nodes also have a file area with downloadable programs and genealogy databases. The nature and size of these depends upon the sysop (as the individual BB "systems operator" is called). Some nodes already contain a great deal of genealogical data, as exemplified by the *Roots* node in San Francisco. The sysop, Brian Mavrogeorge, has developed query indexes (i.e., containing all ancestral names queried about) for the New England, New York, Ohio, Iowa, Pennsylvania, Indiana, Nebraska, California and national genealogical society magazines. (Besides searching it online, you can buy this data in printed or diskette form from him: 89 Stoneybrook, San Francisco, CA 94112.)

A *tiny-tafel* computer-genealogy format, recently tested on the *CommSoft* node in Mountain View, California, allows you to easily upload a summary of the surnames and associated places and time-periods you are researching. It has instant match and automatic scanning features to quickly track down others within the BB system who are researching the same families. This tafel-matching system is now beginning to be implemented by other of the system nodes, a majority of which may offer this service before the end of 1987. *CommSoft* will soon be releasing software (free or at-cost to registered *Roots II*users) to automatically generate tiny-tafels from a genealogical database. (They are are also developing another tafel-generating program for PAF users.)

> **Judging from how many have accessed the new genealogical bulletin boards, genealogists are now becoming active telecommunication users.**

ADDITIONAL CONSUMER GUIDELINES

o   A good local dealership makes it easier to straighten out possible problems face-to-face. Many retail stores, however, do not offer adequate service. We often buy from mail order dealers because of their low prices; but some of these are unscrupulous. In either case, then, minimize risk by checking with user-groups as to an individual firm's service reputation. Ideal would be a local store owner/manager who is honest, knowledgeable and helpful. (Salemen, unfortunately, if good, usually turn over rapidly.) As we have talked with people in different areas of the country, dealer support appears to vary considerably, both from dealer to dealer, and area to area.

o   Alternatively, then, look for toll-free *trouble-shooting* service numbers that make possible immediate help. There are also modem-accessed BB's with technical information and solutions to previous problems posted. Many companies now offer one or the other of these services. Check these options out by in advance to make sure they are good. If so, they may well be worth a little extra in paying for otherwise comparable equipment.

> **A (local or mail order) firm's reputation may vary from poor to quite good. This should be a deciding criterion, even above price considerations.**

---

o   Consider having a mail-order purchase delivered C.O.D. This may save you money (you won't be charged interest on a credit card while waiting for what may turn out to be a long arrival). Also, because irreputable firms may not be willing to so deliver (thus exposing themselves). And finally, because careful inspection of purchases before accepting delivery at least will protect you from obviously shoddy or damaged equipment

o   Used equipment, as may be located through want ads, or new equipment from defunct companies may not be as economical as you'd think. We have noted many want-ads asking more for used equipment than a newer, more powerful system would cost!

Always check out needed additional costs (such as service, support, and upgrading options), therefore, before judging how "good" a deal really is.

o $1,000-2,000 is today's lower price range for obtaining a new and powerful system, including PC, printer, software, lots of memory, and including (in many cases) even a hard disk. If capable of following directions and handling a screwdriver, then for $500-600 or less, and in a couple hours time, you can put together your own 640K IBM-XT Clone. (Some current articles we have seen provide specifics.)

o   Plan to work your equipment hard for 2-5 years. If still satisfactory for your needs, just replace parts as needed to keep it going. Or, as you may find your computer-genealogy system expanding considerably, use add-on memory and storage options (assuming that you wisely allowed for this by buying a system with a sufficient number of expansion slots in the first place). You may even want to replace it with a more powerful new system, often for less than what you paid the first time around. Use your system for more than just genealogy for a cost-efficient purchase. In fact, some may want to do as we have, and use these additional options to pay the cost of your PC. Then your genealogy use ends up free.

SUMMARY

This chapter has presented the advantages possible through computerization, and *how-to's* for obtaining a system best suited to your needs. Computers and software have become more useful and easier to use. However, a price (time and learning, as well as money) still must be paid to enjoy possible benefits and before you'll be able to start concentrating once more on genealogy rather than computing.

We trust our assessment of these costs and benefits will help you make a competetent decision as to whether or not computerization presently offers you a good alternative. If it does, don't be afraid to "go for it." If not, realize that technological advances to help genealogists are going to continue, and the *price-to-power* ratio will keep dropping. So keep your records well-organized in anticipation of the day when you, too, will be ready to enjoy these benefits.

Additionally, keeping errors, or *garbage*, out of our records is always a major concern, whether by hand or machine.

So even if you never automate your system, you will at least want to conduct your research taking into account this computer jargon and truism: GIGO (i.e., Garbage In, Garbage Out).

Finally, expect to enjoy substantial progress in your genealogy system as you are fortunate enough to combine the potential speed, versatility and accuracy of computer technology with correctly-applied research principles.

Chapter 5. CHOOSING A LINE TO RESEARCH

We now invite you to study the *Research Procedure Chart* found in Appendix A, summarizing a logical, effective, step-by-step sequence for conducting research. Earlier chapters have covered beginning steps. We now want to discuss Step #3A, or how to choose a line to research. Notice that choosing a line to research comes after organization and compilation of home and family sources, and after having talked with at least the older family members in *all* branches of the family. This is advisable, first, because obviously a deceased relative cannot be called back to give you information. Second, learning something about each family line obviously helps you make a better researching choice.

Plan to research but one line at a time, unless two or more families resided together in the same place and time period. In that case, it makes sense to research these neighboring families together. It is also best to research your easiest lines first. The experience and knowledge gained in doing straight-forward research will enable you to late tackle more difficult lines with greater effectiveness. Factors influencing difficulty of research, and therefore to be considered in your choice, are as follows:

LANGUAGE

Unless you have the ready help of a translator, an unknown language increases research difficulty (although there are some tools to help overcome this handicap. See Chapter 14).

DISTANCE

Researching a line far from your residence often makes it harder and more expensive to obtain the necessary records for your examination. There will be exceptions, of course. A large genealogical collection containing many of the records you need may be close. Even a nearby small branch genealogical library will be sufficient when the desired records have already been microfilmed by the GSU. For others, travelling may be a looked-forward-to possibility, while many in the near future doubtless will take advantage of telecommunications as a research medium. Otherwise, we advise you to first research those families who resided closest to your present residence.

> **Begin by researching your easiest lines first, and later you'll be able to bettter deal with more difficult research problems.**

AVAILABLE RECORDS

Those times and places with important records still existing should be easiest to research. Conversely, those places without important records are the most difficult to research. For example, parts of tidewater and eastern Virginia constitute a "burned-out" section for genealogists. Valuable early civil records were gathered and removed to Richmond for "safe-keeping" during the Civil War, just before it was razed by the Union army! At least partly due to the Civil War, in fact, it is generally true for United States research that the farther south your ancestors lived, the harder it may be to locate needed records. Early New England records, in contrast, are generally quite good.

Additionally, many individual churches, court houses, and homes flooded or burned; the records thereby destroyed. Sometimes a county clerk or minister was careless, or had insufficient room to keep the records on his courthouse or church premises. The records may then have ended up in cubbyholes, attics, or garbage cans; to be later destroyed by rodents or incinerators or, maybe (we can always hope this is the case for our families!) rediscovered and published many years later.

Obviously, if you have a choice between researching families with good records and families without, you should choose the former. And if you don't learn there is a dearth of records until after beginning research, don't be afraid to change your mind at that point. Your examination of the *Locality Catalog* of the GSU (showing, as it does, the specific records microfilmed for each area) should be quite helpful in allowing you to compare locations for this factor.

MOBILITY

Nomadic groups are invariably harder to trace than stay-at-home farmers. Thus, if your mom's side of the family has been in the town where you now live for five generations, then her line should be easier to research than your dad's family if the latter has moved across county or state lines at least once each generation. Once your lines have been traced back to the "old country," both nomadic and farming groups are likewise found there. Learning which of these most likely contained your ancestors will often become quite obvious upon study of the local history; this is one important reason we will later recommend your investigating these factors preliminary to beginning research.

Cross-country migration was quite common in America, especially in the era following the Revolutionary War. This, together with the scanty family information provided by the pre-1850 census records, have resulted in the decades of 1790-1850 being labelled the "black-out" period. In general, it has proven to be the most difficult era in which to conduct research in this country. The AIS and other census indexes, fortunately, have recently helped relieve some of the gloom associated with researching this time-period; and numerous (some now published and indexed) Revolutionary War pension applications likewise make it posssible to trace many of these families, sometimes for two-three generations following that war service.

> **Genealogy was considered unpatriotic during our Revolutionary Era!**

SOCIAL STATUS

The more prominent a family, the more likely records were kept. Education and resulting literacy, for example, were almost always limited to the upper classes. This class factor will normally have an increasing effect the farther back in time you research. Thus, by the time of the Middle Ages, only nobility and royal lines have been researched with any degree of success in Europe.

UNCOOPERATIVE FAMILY AND "FAMILY MYTHS"

Some lines may be difficult to research due to *family skeletons* in the closet. Because of the aura time lends, as well as today's prevailing notions of tolerance and "anything goes," most today would not be upset (in fact, might even regard it as quite romantic) to discover among their ancestors a grandfather who was a horse-thief, or a grandmother who ran off with a scalawag. Yet certainly some today, and many more among previous generations raised in a more conforming atmosphere, would feel differently. Thus, the ability to learn certain facts some family members want(ed) to keep hidden is necessary to research certain lines.

Different from *family skeletons*, yet resulting in similar kinds of problems, are what we shall term *social desirability* factors. Royal lines seem to have always been desirable. Indeed, desire to link up to one provided the main motivation, historically, for most Europeans interested in genealogy. Consequently, many Americans during our Revolutionary Era considered an interest in genealogy as akin to the European aristocratic tradition and, therefore, as somehow unpatriotic. This accounts for something of a general genealogical set-back for this time-period. Many long-held family trees (including some belonging to this country's distinguished leaders) were lost as a result.

Such *social desirability* factors are more complex today than in the past. Many, and especially of the older generation, retain the traditional interest in royalty. Yet the desire of many modern Americans to find an *Indian Princess* or *Chief* among their ancestors certainly demonstrates an attitude strikingly different than was commonly held even earlier in this century. And a recent UPI dispatch also informs us that Australians who can trace their heritage back to an immigrant prisoner ancestor, have founded special societies for themselves, similar in nature to our DAR.

(Of course, as has been shown by historians, no stigma need be attached to the prisoner, or indentured servant, immigrants. A convict may have been transported for as small an offense as stealing a handkerchief, or trapping a duck on land owned by nobility; while many indentured servants were simply younger sons unable to inherit property under the then-prevailing British system of primogeniture. Although many of these latter came from the yeomanry and peasant classes, others were of aristocratic families. Many "made good," as our own Virginia research verifies.)

Lastly, and further complicating the situation is the recent *ethnic pride* phenomenon. At least two important points emerge as we consider such topics. The first is philisophical. While genealogy is surely a great source of self-knowledge and identity; we also share the convictions of these genealogists:

> "Genealogy truly is a leveler. . . ., and its pursuit should lead one to be tolerant of others [in learning] how tangled and intermingled all our pedigrees are." --David Pratt.   "Possibly one of the incidental functions of genealogical study is to chasten family pride, and to make us more conscious of the essential unity of the great human family." --Donald Jacobus.

The other point to be noted is more practically linked to your research. Human nature being what it is, many have been, and still may be, more motivated to link up to certain *desirable* ancestors, than to portray a verified family history. This will help you appreciate at least one important reason why, to ensure accuracy, evidence from original sources is needed to corroborate any and all genealogical statements found in published or family sources.

DUPLICATION

Of course you want to strenuously avoid the useless waste of your time and effort in researching the same records for the same names as someone else has previously done. Previously given suggestions, such as communicating with all known relatives to find out what family research exists, and then checking the *IGI*, *Family Registry*, and (when it becomes available) the *Ancestral File*, will help you avoid the unfortunately common problem of duplication. The *Genealogical Research Directory*, published annually since 1983 and found in many libraries, may also help for this purpose. The most recent, 1986, edition contains over 100,000 research enquiries from 25 different countries.

COMMON NAMES

The last general factor making research difficult is dealing with a very common surname. As was explained in Chapter 3, each time an entry is found with the surname you're researching, you will want to make record of it. This is necessary to determine which of all those Smiths are actually *your* Smiths, and so requires your taking many more notes than you otherwise would. An even more important disadvantage is the increased likelihood of mistaken identity.

This warning against starting off your research with a common surname is especially valid if the family used common first names as well. Fortunately, some families with common surnames have made themselves more identifiable by the use of distinctive first, or Christian, names. Because these Christian names were usually traditional names carried on through successive generations (see Chapter 14) this will often make your search easier.

SUMMARY

Examine your family tree to learn which lines should be easiest to research. An easy line will have many existing, readable records going back for several generations in a location near you; have distinctive names; be of a higher social class; and have few family skeletons. If, using these criteria, there are no easy lines, patience with your task will surely be necessary. But you may yet enjoy success as you learn and adhere to correct genealogical research principles.

Expect to encounter some rough–going in tracing a family that was nomadic, lived far from your present residence, had common names, was of a lower social class, or lived in an area suffering extensive record loss.

Chapter 6. USING LIBRARIES

Library collections of local histories, genealogies, bibliographies, and maps/atlases are treasure houses for the family historian. Almost every nation, state, or province has one or more large repository where much of its early records have been gathered, such as a *State Archive* (Appendix B of *The Source*, referenced in Chapter 7, lists each of our 50 State Archives).

Large public or university libraries may also have excellent sources (Dallas, Denver, San Franciso, Los Angeles, and Seattle, exemplify public libraries with extra-large genealogical collections; and the South Caroliniana Library in Columbia, South Carolina, exemplifies a university library with such). There are even special libraries completely devoted to genealogy, such as the DAR Libraries in Oklahoma City, Oklahoma, and Alliance, Nebraska; and the Filson Club Library in Louisville, Kentucky. Chapter 15 contains a list of several other extra-large and helpful collections. But don't overlook even small libraries in the ancestral hometown. Depending on the area, these may even prove to be the most helpful of all.

HOW-TO'S OF LIBRARY RESEARCH

One of us works at a large Virginia university. We have never seen its library name listed with other good genealogical repositories, nor is there a section of the library labelled *Genealogy*, as such. From our own experience, however, we know it to contain a wealth of research material, especially excellent for this state. This is probably true of most all large academic or public libraries. Unfortunately, many are thwarted in library searching, lacking needed skills.

> **Guided tours offer a fast way to learn what all a library includes.**

Students in our genealogy classes invariably express great satisfaction when, through guided tour, they learn just how to find the many genealogical materials available. Because guided tours provide potentially the fastest way to learn just what is included in a particular collection, ask about these in any library where you expect to do much research. Alternatively, you may want to enlist the aid of a friend, family member, or a cooperative local librarian to teach you needed skills of being able to: (1) use the card or online catalog, (2) find things by call number, (3) and use the pertinant indexes, catalogs, and special collections.

Card Catalog : There are three basic approaches to the card catalog: (1) by author, (2) by title, and (3) by subject. In addition, some genealogical libraries have other files: (4) by locality and (5) by surnames. For the beginning genealogist, as well as for anybody investigating a field new to them, the subject (and locality or surname if available) approach is usually the most productive. Begin by going to these sections of the card catalog and there look up the surname(s), location(s), or any other subject(s) on which you need information. (Appendix B has helpful subject-headings.)

Several large libraries are using online or microfiche catalogs to replace card catalogs. Do not be scared off by this trend toward automation in libraries. Automated systems make it possible to find things more easily and completely, especially in a very large collection. Look for the written instructions generally available at the computer terminals.

Call Number: In the upper left-hand corner of each catalog card is the call number, i.e., the number and letter information coding the location of a book within the collection. Copy down complete call numbers for each item you want to examine. As you gain experience at finding things by call number you'll find this is a logical (although certainly not always obvious) way of arranging the books, so that books of like subject are grouped together. Most call numbers have two parts. The first part groups the books by the subject, and the second part arranges a book within a subject alphabetically by the main entry; in most cases, this is the author. The classification systems used by libraries aren't all identical; so ask the librarian for directions until you become experienced.

Some genealogy books pose the problem of being shelved "out of sequence." This is because books considered as reference works are shelved in a separate reference area; others, considered rare or fragile are likewise shelved in yet another special location for protection. These different locations are usually noted by headings such as *ref* or *spec* on the catalog card; but if you can't find a book in its supposed location, or are otherwise unsuccessful, don't hesitate to ask a librarian for help (the supervisor of the genealogy and local history collection is generally the most informed for your purposes).

Indexes: Just as card or online catalogs enable you to locate desired books, so do indexes enable you to find desired subjects of interest within those books, as well as within periodicals, newspapers, and other sources. There are indispensible subject and name indexes in all major libraries, covering sources as diverse as censuses, newspaper obituaries, or published and unpublished journals and manuscripts. Because an index including some of your ancestral names may offer much help, and because so many of these are being compiled, you may even want to review all new possibilities with the librarian every several months or so.

Some helpful indexes found in many large libraries are listed in Chapter 7's Bibliography; but be aware of the possibility of indexes covering the smaller locale you wish to research. Much excellent work, for example, is being done by local and state genealogical societies in gathering pertinant, and often widely-scattered, materials; these are then published in their periodicals, as detailed in our next chapter.

Of course, indexes found at the end of books can also be helpful. But don't rely overly on them; you may easily miss important data if you do no more than rapidly skim through an index. To make best use of any indexed book, first read the book's prefatory material, as well as the first page of the index. Qualifications given there are often necessary to use the book and its index effectively. You may thus discover, for example, that certain sections of the book were not indexed (e.g., appendixes, sections containing long lists of names, or material already alphabetically arranged) and so you would need to examine these sections separately. Then try looking up in the index a few items found within the text, as a check to see how complete the index is. Indexes in older books tend to leave out much. If that is so, you'll need to carefully examine the table of contents to see which parts may be worth searching on a page by page basis.

Targetted Approach: Knowing how to use card catalogs, indexes, and such, will help only to the extent you are thorough in looking for the names, locations, and any other topics relevant to your research. To ensure thoroughness, use a targetted approach by first aiming for the "bull's eye," i.e., your particular family in their specific location.

Use a systematic targetted approach to ensure thorough research.

For instance, if you're interested in the Cyrus Brown family residing in Hard Rock, Sassafrass County, Kansas, then the bull's-eye name and place for your search would be Cyrus Brown and Hard Rock, Kansas. If the card catalog gives no headings for Cyrus Brown or Hard Rock, then expand the target by looking for any members of the Brown family in Sassafrass County; these may include relatives of your Cyrus.

If you find nothing on Browns in Sassafrass County, then enlarge your target again and check for information on any Brown family in Kansas. There may be many such books, yet, it shouldn't be too difficult to check each index for a Cyrus.

If still unsuccessful, try searching for other related names. For example, you know his wife's maiden surname was Funk, his mother-in-law's maiden name was Ethel Showalter and his daughter married Bill Read. These additional names expand your research possibilities because any book or index entry pertaining to the Kansas Funks, Showalters, or Reads might also include information or clues helpful in your Cyrus Brown investigation.

Targets can be expanded whenever you learn of in-laws or suspected relatives. These include neighbors of the same surname(s), or whose names are associated with them in public or family records (such as witnesses or sponsors to your family's deeds, wills, or christenings). Also, if your Browns are found in the Hard Rock town cemetery buried together with Humphreys, again suspect a family relationship, and include their name as another to research.

LIBRARY GENEALOGICAL BIBLIOGRAPHIES

The directions provided in this chapter are to acquaint you with the *hows* of library research. The *whats*, i.e., what specific tools and information sources will be waiting for you at the library, will be detailed in later chapters. But in talking to the librarian, be sure to inquire early as to whether the library has assembled a pamphlet or bibliography listing its genealogical sources.

In some cases large libraries may even put out instruction sheets or books on how to do genealogy, usually with special emphasis upon their collection. This is true of many of the LDSGL's research aids. As another example, the New York State Library has put out a helpful book entitled, *Gateway to America: Genealogical Research in the New York State Library*. This, of course, would especially benefit those of New York ancestry with access to that library. Anytime you will be travelling some distance to accomplish research in a collection, try to locate and study such a guide or bibliography before your trip (if necessary, making a phone-call, or sending them an SASE, to obtain that information).

OBTAINING INFORMATION FROM OTHER LIBRARIES

Sometimes, while checking in various indexes or bibliographies, you will find reference to a book with information on your families, or that may otherwise help you, that is not held by your local libraries. If so, we suggest you first check two sources to be found at the GSU or its branches. One of these is the soon-to-be available microfiche collection, *100 Most Used Books* (containing the full text of many helpful published genealogical sources). If not in that collection, then check the GLC as explained in Chapter 2. It is valuable not only because covering a very large collection, but also because the GSU provides reasonable photocopy service by mail through forms available at its branch genealogical libraries. If the source you want is unavailable through the GSU, check the latest edition of *Genealogical and Local History Books in Print* by Nellie Schreiner-Yantis. The 4th, 1985, edition (2 volumes; over 1,700 pages) has genealogical titles listed by both subject and locality with full ordering information (i.e., price, and address of vendor).

Another option is to ask your local public or academic librarian to check on obtaining the desired book from another library. Interlibrary loan (ILL) currently provides a good method for borrowing many, but not all (as most collections refuse to loan or photocopy rare or fragile) genealogical books. Smaller libraries are generally more reasonably priced; a prestigious academic library, for instance, may routinely charge $15 for processing an ILL request that a small public library would supply free. Our final chapter has a sample letter addressed to a reference librarian; this is often a good person to query if you are having problems learning what published sources are available for a locality.

Getting photocopies of a periodical article is usually expensive. Exceptions are the services provided by the GSU and by *Heritage Quest* magazine, to be explained in our next chapter.

SCHOLARLY MICROPUBLISHING

Scholarly micropublishing (i.e., publication of microfilms and microfiche collections) is not new. Nevertheless, it has recently become a large industry and it greatly increases the results possible from your library research. For it is in the field of history (American history is especially popular) where we find so many of these collections. Because they are expensive, the biggest of these collections are found only in larger libraries. Some of these collections are quite new; others that have been around for several years are still being added to. We will here list just a sampling of some that may interest you:

o   *Genealogy and Local History* is an ambitious ongoing collection being done by University Microfilms International; its most recent sections cover the state of New York in the 19th Century and earlier.

o   *Genealogy and Family History* being issued by a microform press in England, covers Great Britain.

o   *Genealogical and Biographical Research*, a catalog issued by the National Archives to describe its huge microform holdings in this area.

o   *Massachusetts Vital Records* is another ongoing set; this one being done by the Holbrook Research Institute. When finished, it will reproduce the original birth, marriage and death manuscript records for some 375 townships in Massachusetts through 1895.

o   *The Immigrant in America* covers the period 1789-1929 and is being done by Research Publications (also responsible for issuing many *City Directories* another valuable research resource.

AUTOMATED DEVELOPMENTS IN LIBRARY RESEARCH

As earlier mentioned, libraries and information centers are tending towards automation with resulting benefits to the user. First, photcopy machines, then automated catalogs, and now an entirely new service that should eventually have tremendous impact on genealogical research. This service is using telecommunications to search online databases.

One of us does professional online searching in the sciences, and is impressed with some of the advantages thereby made possible. Besides a substantial increase in speed and accuracy, there is increased *precision* made possible by specific field searching, and the use of boolean logic and proximity operators. For example, if interested in the city of New York for only a two year time-period, a manual search would normally require you to wade through much other data as well in order to find the specifics relevant to your search. But in a computer search you could combine terms to limit your findings to precisely what is needed, no more. Say, for example: *New York City, 1850–1852*, and *not Irish*.

Another important advantage is the far greater number of *access points* possible in a computerized database. This means that when you look for the name *Funk* in a computerized *Who's Who*, for example, you will find more than just those few notables indexed under this surname. For now you can locate any Funks mentioned anywhere within the database. For example, a spouse or mother whose maiden or middle name is Funk, an in-law Funk, a work associate named Funk, etc. This obviously expands your research possibilites.

Already most university libraries can search huge national and international engineering, science, business, legal, or medical databases for a fee. Using online searching techniques it is possible within a few minutes to obtain a customized and completely updated list of references pertaining to a desired specific topic. This list might include items that would otherwise require days or even weeks of manual searching to uncover, as well as contain other items that formerly might only be accidentally uncovered. Of course, such searching is only possible because the pertinent information has already been assembled into comprehensive databases.

A few of these databases contain biography and history and may thus be used to quickly locate facts pertinent to your research. Furthermore, the large and well-known commercial online vendor, *Dialog*, has just recently added three of the best of these databases to their widely-available and low cost online system for home computer users, *Knowledge Index*.

The databases on *Knowledge Index* of most interest to genealogists thus now include: *Marquis' Who's Who, Historical Abstracts* (covers history and local history of areas outside the United States and Canada), *American: History and Life* (covers history and local history of the United States and Canada), and *Dissertation Abstracts*. This latter covers doctoral dissertations awarded by most universities in the United States and Canada in all academic areas, including local and regional history. (It does not, unfortunately, include those submitted at the University of Chicago, Harvard University, or M.I.T.)

This is great news. For one thing, *Knowledge Index* is easy to use, being designed specifically for the home computerist. For another, it costs only about $24 per connect hour. This is quite economical when you realize that in just fifteen minutes to 1/2 hour, you may be able to accomplish as much searching as might otherwise require many hours or even days! You will need a computer and modem to take advantage of this service. If you live close to a telephone network node, then your phone-line use will be free. Call 800-3-DIALOG to learn more details.

For historical background, "Knowledge Index" now provides fast, efficient and economical research of historical and biographical databases.

To this point there are no comparable genealogical online databases. Yet we are encouraged as to what lies in the near future because of recent remarkable developments in information storage. The Library of Congress, for instance, to preserve rapidly deteriorating books and journals, has developed a pilot project using high technologies to digitize and photograph maps, pictures, books, and journals, and then to store these on optical discs. The GSU, as we have seen, is already actively using *CD-ROM in conjunction with its online technology. (And such hybrid systems, by accessing both online and offline databases, would indeed seem most useful of all.)

Such developments are exciting, as it means that old and valuable biographies, genealogies, and local histories should eventually be retrievable over phone lines by other libraries and by home computers, in the same way that business and engineering databases are at present. Other databases may be available *offline*, i.e., on laser disc or CD-ROM. These advances are coming rapidly, and it may not be long before you need to periodically check with your librarian about the availability of online and offline databases, even as you now need to check with them about newly published micro-collections and books.

Few are able to keep current in the field of information technology. Available systems already have the potential to store all of the world's written records within just one room. Indeed, the challenge of the future may not be our present one of finding *enough* information on genealogical research projects. Rather, the challenge may be in finding *too much*, calling for a whole new set of research techniques. This both sparks the imagination and boggles the mind as we attempt to contemplate what genealogical searching may be like in the future as upgraded information storage and retrieval systems become more fully implemented.

In summary, we have much to look forward to. For as the advances now occurring within laserdisc technology are combined with developing abilities to digitize and make written records machine-readable, it will simply be a matter of some time and "doing it," before much genealogical data that is now difficult to find, or even virtually unretrievable, will become readily, even instantaneously, accessible.

SUMMARY

You certainly want to be on good terms with, if not a good friend of your reference librarian, as well as be familiar with some simple library searching techniques. Although recent information technology developments promise exciting possibilities for the future, yet much good help already exists, and the following chapter details some of these important tools.

Chapter 7. COMPILED SOURCES; SOCIETIES & MAGAZINES

Compiled sources are books resulting from another person's research. Such a book can be valuable to you, *if* the compiler checked into original records concerning any of your relatives, and especially *if* the work was accurately done. It will be even more valuable if the work is also comprehensive, i.e., covers most or all available relevant sources. Needless to say, much variation exists among compiled sources as to how well they fulfill these criteria.

The ideal possibility, then, is to discover some meticulous, experienced researcher has carefully examined all pertinent sources for a family you wanted to investigate, and has accurately published the research results. This will be rare. Yet even in the opposite case, where a published work is based on poorly-compiled and inadequately documented research, it may yet be a valuable source. Perhaps, for example, the compiler had access to sources relevant to your family history long since lost, or talked with people long since deceased.

Many compiled sources exist. They generally contain an abundance of data that provides at least some clues, if not a good basis, for your research. Of course, *all* compiled sources run the risk of at least transcribing or typographical errors. Our next chapter explains the reasons for preferring evidence gleaned from primary over secondary sources. Compiled sources, by definition, fall into the latter category.

GENEALOGIES AND FAMILY HISTORIES

Genealogies and family histories are important: they should be searched not only to prevent duplication of research, but to gather helpful information on direct and related lines. Unfortunately, most old, and even some more recent, genealogies and family histories were written by authors careless in their research. Understanding that genealogy is a field to be pursued with the same painstaking care for accuracy and documentation as in other fields of scholarship is a notion that, unfortunately, has yet to be generally accepted even today. Additionally, the author may not have had ready access to the many excellent genealogical and historical sources only recently available.

Because many published genealogies and family histories are poorly done, it is helpful to study a well-done one first. Then you can better evaluate those pertaining to your family. Ask your librarian or a genealogist to recommend a good one in your local library. You will be skeptical, naturally, of unsupported published reports of famous long-age ancestors. Pay special notice, however, to facts about then-living family members: generally, the closer the time and relationship, the more reliable the evidence.

Those doing foreign research will also want to look for these sources: some very good ones exist. Germany provides an excellent example with its many published and unpublished *Ortssippenbücher (local clan books)*. These were compiled in the 1930's for racial-political reasons by local genealogists using card cataloged vital entries from the German parish registers (dating as far back as the 1600's) and the local register offices (for the 1875-1930 era). These books in general conform to such high standards of accuracy that demographers and other scholars have been able to use them to conduct modern computerized studies. (More than 100 have been published since 1937. Write the mayor or local minister to learn if such a book, published or unpublished, exists for a community of interest.)

LOCAL HISTORIES

Local histories of towns, counties, and regions, besides being good sources to obtain historical and geographical background, may have biographical sections. Examine these for your names. Local histories again range from excellent to poor, so you'll need to use good judgment, as well as the previously-suggested comparison approach, to properly evaluate them. Because many of these histories and genealogies are old, and the facts are often based on reports of then-living informants, reading them is almost like interviewing people who lived some generations ago. Don't overlook that opportunity.

BIOGRAPHICAL WORKS

o   Herbert, M.C. and McNeil, B. *Biography and Genealogy Master Index*, 2nd ed. with supplements, 1981-5. Gale Research Co., Detroit, MI: 1985. (A widely-found reference indexing almost *five million* biographies!)

o   Filby, P. Wm. *American and British Genealogy and Heraldry : a Selected List of Books*, 3rd ed. Boston: New England Historic Genealogical Society, and *Supplement* (covers 1982-4) 1983-5. (Among its listings are local biographical sources; while you have it, check through its other excellent helps. Excellent reference for American, including Latin American, Canadian, and British research, and good for many other countries.

Because of the abundance of biographies available, check this source even if you are unaware of any "famous" people in your immediate family. After all, there may easily be someone worthy of biographical mention in a branch with which you're less familiar.

COMPILED REGISTERS and DIRECTORIES

Another potentially valuable reference to examine consists of compiled registers, directories, and comparable works for different sections, states, organizations (e.g., U.S. Army), and groups (e.g. early New England settlers). Because these compilations are normally based on original records and done by experienced compilers, their reliability and accuracy is often better than other compiled sources.

LOCAL HISTORICAL SOCIETIES/MAGAZINES, GENEALOGY MAGAZINES

Local genealogical and historical societies with their associated periodicals are potentially very good sources. Much of the current research findings are published in these, as well as in certain larger magazines. These periodicals may also include needed up-dates as to what additional compiled sources and indexes for the area are being published. Consider joining a society, or subscribing to the particular magazine, best covering your area of concern. In many of the latter you will be able to publish free queries about your families; this is often fruitful. *Genealogical Societies & Historical Societies*, 1985, by J. Conrad contains world-wide society listings.

One purpose of the local genealogical or historical societies is to help people there conducting genealogical research in their area. And affiliation thus gives you the opportunity to meet the genealogists who are knowledgable and experienced in the very area of your interest. This can be quite helpful; for instance, if you become "stuck" in your research, or don't know how to exactly interpret some findings. Societies may also sponsor conferences or seminars providing good help.

The Genealogical Helper, the largest genealogical magazine, is generally a good source to learn of newly published genealogical works for all areas. (Published by Everton Publishers, Inc. 3223 S. Main St., Nibley, UT 84321. $17/yr, 6 issues; $4.50/single issue. Mr. Schweitzer in his *Genealogical Source Handbook*, pp.97-100, suggests a systematic means for subscribers to use its contents in their research.)

A list of some large journals in the USA is found in Appendix F, but there are numerous more periodicals, including several hundred relatively unknown outside their small memberships, being published by family organizations or small local societies. Further, these have tended to lack indexes. Thus, laborious page by page searching is often necessary to uncover their "hidden" data. The task of tracking down all of these that may possibly be producing relevant material for you, let alone then checking through them, to this point has thus been so formidable as to be a practically impossible task.

Fortunately, various sources are helping somewhat in the compilation of this important information. One of these is *Heritage Quest*. Among other things this magazine computer indexes pertinent articles out of numerous genealogical and local history periodicals, giving precedence to the current issues. It also provides a helpful, reasonably-priced article copy service. Copying a 7 page article, for example, would cost you only an SASE and $2.40 or $3.40 (respective costs for a member or non-member). Another growing computerized, indexed collection of ancestral queries is mentioned on page 34.

Many helpful periodicals are also published abroad. *The Federation of Family History Societies in the United Kingdom* (Chapter 15 for address) is a good source to learn particulars on many worldwide organizations with their journals. Because there are again great differences in quality among periodicals, we suggest you carefully peruse some well-done ones first. *The New England Historic Genealogical Register* and the *National Genealogical Society Quarterly* are journals published by well-known societies whose articles consistently stress or exemplify high standards of accuracy in research.

One of us in doing extensive Virginia research has been much aided through use of magazine indexes. Several early important genealogical magazines for this state were indexed by Swem's *Virginia Historical Index*; the *The Virginia Genealogist*, a fine journal for that state has an index covering its first 20 years; and other current Viriginia newsletters put out yearly indexes to their material.

NEWSPAPERS

Newspaper collections for your ancestor's locality are another valuable resource; some are even indexed. Ask your librarian specifically about these as microfilms are sometimes hard to find in the card catalog. Of course, newspapers as secondary sources are subject to error; however, they may sometimes be the only remaining source of certain facts. Obituary notices are a good example. And further clues may also be found through birth, engagement or marriage announcements; news items; or even ads. Here, for instance, is an advertisement that supplied us with secondary evidence about the English origins of an early Hilliard/Hollier family we researched. (This is data often difficult to uncover for early colonists). It originally appeared in a 1771 *Virginia Gazette*, and was found through Swem's *Virginia Historical Index*.

If any of the descendants of John Hellier, who came to Virginia many years ago, from Bristol, in Great Britain, and settled in the Freshes of the Rappahannock River, will apply to me in Fredericksburg (Virginia.), they will be informed of a particular inquiry made after them, perhaps much to their advantage. . .I have heard of a family of the name of "Hilliard," who came from Bristol, and formerly settled in the neighborhood of the late Col. Turner, on the Rappahannock. If any of that family are alive, perhaps they may reconcile the difference of the name from convincing circumstances, as there is so great a similitude in name. ---(inserted by Roger Dixon)

GENEALOGICAL COLUMNS

Another compiled source that might prove to be of worth to you are the genealogical columns appearing in newspapers. Some of these date back a long ways; e.g., the *Boston Transcript*, which compiled great amounts of information throughout the nineteenth century. It has since been indexed and microfilmed (available through the GSU and elsewhere). Many current newspapers carry valuable genealogical columns. One source for locating these is *List of Newspapers with Genealogical Query Columns* by J. Konrad, up-to-date as of 1984, and another is the most current Aug-Sept issue of the *Stagecoach Library Bulletin*, published by Gary T. Hawbaker, PO Box 207, Hershey, PA 17033. Here is a recent sample-excerpt:

o *Lineage and Letters*, Mrs. Emma Linder, The Southern Democrat, Cherry Hill Farm, Rt. 4, Bx 259, Oneonta, AL 35121; accepts *general* queries; free; 7th yr.

Most areas have newspapers carrying genealogical columns; when finding one for your location of interest, consider sending them a query about your family. It may well attract the attention of a distant relative still living in your ancestral location, or of a local genealogist who is likely to read such columns. These are the people with possible answers to your questions.

SUMMARY

There are many valuable, helpful tools found in libraries and through the local genealogical societies and their periodicals. Seek to make full use of these, including compiled sources, at this point. The following Bibliography includes titles of many good references, but look also for those relating to your more specific areas of interest, and see Appendix F for large journals in this country.

BIBLIOGRAPHY: 1. BIBLIOGRAPHIES AND INDEXES

Library of Congress. *Library of Congress Catalog. Books: Subjects.* . . ., 1950-

_____.*United States Local Histories in the Library of Congress: A Bibliography.* 4 vol. Marion J. Kaminkow. Ed. Baltimore: Magna Carta Book Co., 1975.

_____. *Genealogies in the Library of Congress: A Bibliography.* Supplement, 3 vol. 1972-1977. Marion J. Kaminkow. Ed. Baltimore: Magna Carta Book Co., 1977.

Kaminkow, Marion J., ed. *A Complement to Genealogies in the Library of Congress: A Bibliography.* Baltimore: Magna Carta Book Co., 1981. (20,000 family histories)

New York Public Library. *Dictionary Catalog of the Local History and Genealogy Division.* 20 vols. Boston: G.K. Hall, 1974. (Additions since 1972 have been included in *Dictionary Catalog of the Research Libraries.*)

Brown, Mary J. *Handy Index to the Holdings of the Genealogical Society of Utah: Counties of the United States.* 2nd ed. Everton Publishers, Inc., 1980.

U.S. National Archives and Records Service. *Guide to Genealogical Research in the National Archives.* National Archives Trust Fund Board. Rev. 1983.

Newberry Library. Chicago. *The Genealogical Index.* 4 vols. Boston: G.K. Hall. 1960.

(References 500,000+ surnames found in that library thru 1918.)

Haigh, Roger M., ed. *Finding Aids to the Microfilmed Manuscript Collection of the Genealogical Society of Utah*. Univ. of Utah Press, 1978-. Includes several numbers, e.g., *Preliminary Survey of the French/German/Mexican Collection; Descriptive Inventory of the English/New York Collection,* etc.

American Genealogical Index. Fremont Rider, ed. Middletown, CT., Godfrey Mem. Lib., 1942-52. 48 v. Volumes arranged alphabetically by surname; use with the following (being superseded by it):

American Genealogical-Biographical Index to American Genealogical Biographical and Local History Materials. Fremont Rider, ed. V. 1-. 1952-. Middletown, CT., Godfrey Mem. Lib. By spring, 1987, had progressed alphabetically to the letter "R."

Filby, P. Wm. *American and British Genealogy and Heraldry: A Selected List of Books*, 3rd ed. Boston: NEHGS, 1983. (Excellent; see comments made earlier in the chapter.)

Meyer, Mary Keysor, ed. *Directory of Genealogical Societies in the U.S. and Canada, with an Appended List of Independent Genealogical Periodicals*, 5th ed. Pasadena, MD: The Ed., 1984. (addresses, hours, works)

Kirkham, E. Kay. *An Index to Some of the Family Records of the Southern States*. Vol. 1., 1979. *Index to Some of the Bibles and Family Records of the United States*. Vol. 2., 1984 Logan, Utah: Everton Publishers.

Volume 6: *U.S. Biography and Genealogy Index*, part of the *Combined Retrospective Index Set to Journals in History 1838-1974* VA: Carrollton Press, 1977.

The Greenlaw Index of the Holdings of the New England Historic Genealogical Society. 2V. Boston, MA: G.K. Hall & Co, 1980.

Schreiner-Yantis, Netti. *Genealogical and Local History Books in Print*. 4th ed, 1985. (Order from author: 6818 Lois Drive, Springfield, VA 22150.)

Joel Munsell's Sons, Publishers. *Index to American Genealogies*. Baltimore: Gen. Pub. Co. (Repr. of 1900 ed. and supplement to 1908); 1967. Surname index to 15,000 + family histories (mostly New England, Mid-Atlantic) in books and periodicals beginning 1868.

_____. *The American Genealogist, Being a Catalogue of Family Histories*. Detroit: Gale Research Co., 1975. (Repr. of 1900 ed.) Use with preceeding, being in part a bibliography of it.

Bradford, Thomas Lindsley, comp. *Bibliographer's Manual of American History*. (Repr. of a 5 v. 1907-1910 ed.) Detroit: Gale Res. Co., 1968. Microform. NY: AMS Press, 1974.

Filby, P. William. *A Bibliography of American County Histories*. Baltimore: Gen. Pub. Co., 1985. (Includes 5,000 published by Dec., 1984).

2. PERIODICAL INDEXES FOR FINDING FAMILY HISTORY ARTICLES

British Humanities Index. 1962+. London, Library Ass'n. Annual. Good for local history.

Jacobus, Donald L. *Index to Genealogical Periodicals 1932-1953*. Repr. Baltimore: Genealogical Pub. Co., 1973. 3 vols. in 1, covering 1850's-1952.

Waldenmaier, Inez. *Annual Index to Genealogical Periodicals and Family Histories*. vols. for 1956-62. Washington, D.C.: The author, 1956-1962.

Genealogical Periodical Annual Index. 1962+. Bladensburg, MD: Genealogical Recorders. Vols 1-4, ed. Ellen S. Rogers. Vols 5-8, edited by George E. Russell. Vols. 9-12 (1970-1973) not yet published. Vols. 13-15, (1974-1976), edited by Laird C. Towle. Vols. 16-20 (1977-1980) edited by C.M. Mayhew and Laird C. Towle.

Sperry, Kip, Ed. *A Survey of American Genealogical Periodicals and Periodical Indexes*. Gale Gen. & Local History Ser., Vol.3. Detroit: Gale Res. Co., 1978.

_____. *Index to Genealogical Periodical Literature, 1960-1977*. (Indexes published local records, other important sources; but *no* name index.)

The Maryland Historical Society maintains an unpublished cumulative index to the *Maryland Historical Magazine* at 201 W. Monument St, Baltimore, MD 21201.

Swem, Earl Le G., Comp. *Virginia Historical Index*. Roanoke, VA: Stone Printing, 1934-1936. Repr. Northampton, MS: Peter Smith, 1965. 2 v. Name, place, subject index to important Virginia periodicals and compiled sources, through 1930.

Brown, Stuart E. *Virginia Genealogies*. Berryville, VA: Virginia Book Co., 1980. Updates an earlier 1967 volume by this author, and updates Swem for Virginia periodicals.

3. NEWSPAPER BIBLIOGRAPHIES AND INDEXES

U.S. Library of Congress. Catalog Publication Div. *Newspapers in Microform: United States, 1948-1972, 1973-1977; Newspapers in Microform: Foreign Countries, 1948-1972, 1973-1977*; and *Newspapers in Microform 1978-*. Washington, DC: Library of Congress, 1973, 1978, 1979-.

Gregory, Winifred. *American Newspapers, 1821-1936*. Repr. NY: Kraus, 1967.

Brigham, Clarence S. *History and Bibliography of American Newspapers, 1690-1820*. Reprint. Westport, CT.: Greenwood, 1976.

"State Union Lists." In *Library Service for Genealogists*, pp 208-212. J. Carlyle Parker, ed. Gale Gen. and Local History Series, vol. 15. Detroit: Gale Research Co., 1981.

Milner, Anita Cheek. *Newspaper Indexes: a Location and Subject Guide for Researchers*. 3 vol. Metuchen, NJ: Scarecrow Press, 1977, 1979, 1982.

American Library Association; Jr. Members Round Table. *Local Indexes in American Libraries; a Union List of Unpublished Indexes*. Norma O. Ireland, ed. Repr. Boston: Gregg Press, 1972.

Conrad, J. *List of Newspapers with Genealogical Query Columns*, 19 pp, 1984. (In genealogy bookstores).

Chapter 8. EVALUATION AND EVIDENCE

Learning to evaluate is necessary for successful research in *all* fields, and certainly in genealogy. This is step #4 on our Research Procedure Chart in Appendix A.

JUDGING PRINTED SOURCES

Your ability to critically evaluate printed sources will increase as you gain experience in using original records. Yet, again, one of the best ways to gain a feel for *good* or *bad* printed sources is by studying the best of these. Before beginning research in early western Virginia, we were fortunate to talk to a historian who had done extensive research prior to writing her own works. She recommended *Virginia Frontier* by F.B. Kegley as being as accurate as anything she had come across. In all her researching into original records, she had not found mistakes in any of his statements (even though he doesn't always state his sources. As the late Jacobus in his classic, *Genealogy as Pastime and Profession*, states: "I would rather take the unreferenced word of a capable genealogist. . . than to trust an incompetent genealogist with all the references in the world.")

This book greatly helped us by giving good historical background, valuable leads on our families of interest, and by providing us a high standard by which we could judge other printed works. Several books by Patricia G. Johnson, current historian on western Virginia, were also read, used, and appreciated for these same reasons. Her books also contain another benefit found in some of the better current works: detailed referencing to the original documents consulted.

You will provide yourself a good foundation for your later research by reading such *classic* works pertaining to the particular area of your interest. Find out which are recommended by librarians, experienced genealogists, or by the appropriate bibliographies. Rubincam's *Genealogical Research*, Eakle and Cerni's *The Source*, Filby's *American and British Genealogy and Heraldry* (see in Bibliographies) are good examples of the excellent and up-to-date bibliographies for the United States and many other countries you may here utilize.

EVIDENCE

Although it's good to have some idea about the worth of a source in general; but even more important is to correctly evaluate each fact obtained, so as to know how much comparative weight to assign it. Thus, you want to learn how to categorize among the following classifications of evidence: direct or circumstantial, primary or secondary.

Direct and Primary: *Direct* evidence, as the name suggests, answers a question directly. A birth certificate that states where and when the person was born and who the parents were, thus provides direct evidence of a birth date and place and parentage. Or a dated notation of marriage found in a person's journal, again provides direct evidence for the names of the participants and their marriage date.

Primary evidence is recorded at the time of the event, or very closely thereafter, by a trustworthy witness of the event. If the above birth certificate, for example, was made shortly after the birth and signed by the doctor or midwife present, then the birth certificate can be considered primary (as well as direct) evidence for this person's birth date, birth place, mother, and who the father is reported to be (except, perhaps, in the event of an illegitimate birth). If the above journal marriage notation was likewise recorded within a short time of that event, it also provides primary, as well as direct, evidence of that marriage. In all cases, even as in a court of law, we would like to prove our genealogical hypotheses with primary, direct evidence.

> **Whenever possible, support your conclusions by primary and direct evidence.**

Secondary: *Secondary* evidence includes several variations considered less reliable than primary. For example, if the above birth certificate gave parental ages and/or birthplaces, this would be considered secondary, rather than primary, evidence, inasmuch as these facts concerned events occurring some decades earlier. This illustrates how one document may easily be a source of primary evidence for some facts (in this case, birth information about one person) and yet, a secondary source for others (in this case, birth information about his or her parents).

A family Bible in which marriage and birth notations were made sometime after the events would also be considered as secondary evidence for those vital dates. In some cases, at least, you will be able to deduce that some time elapsed between the events and the time of their recording by the the color of ink used (the same color implying that all notations were recorded at the same time), or because the publication date of the Bible is later than some or all of the dates. (You should therefore make note of inkcolor or handwriting variations, and of publication date, as well as of all family data, when recording information taken from a Family Bible.) This falls in the category of secondary evidence made by reliable witnesses to the event, i.e. the parents, but recorded sometime after the time of the event.

Another category of secondary evidence includes events recorded at the time of their occurance, but by somebody who was not an eyewitness. Let's say, for example, you found among some old family letters, one postmarked July 10, 1908, New Haven, Connecticut, signed by a Calvin Hendricks, addressed to a Lona Fewens of St. Louis, Missouri., with a salutation *Dear Sister*, and congratulating her on the birth of her son William two weeks previous. This letter would be direct, but secondary, evidence for the birthdate of that child.

Secondary evidence also includes records made some years after the event by someone who was not an eyewitness to the event, or by an eyewitness judged to be untrustworthy. This kind of evidence, of course, provides the least credible kind of secondary evidence. A pension application by the widow of a Revolutionary War veteran, for instance, might include his birthdate as part of this file. How much credibility do we give it? Because the source was his widow who, presumably, was not an eyewitness to the birth of her husband, and because she is supplying data about an event occuring a whole lifetime previous, this is such secondary evidence. Certainly if we find it in conflict with a birthdate found for him in a town or church register, then, we would certainly record the latter date as better.

And in case this widow supplies their marriage date as part of this same pension file, this also may not be good evidence; for federal legislation during some periods required the widow of a Revolutionary War veteran to have married the deceased soldier prior to his entering military service in order for her to be eligible to receive a pension. If her application was made when such legislation was in effect, then you realize she may have had an ulterior motive for supplying an inauthentic marriage date. Because it would have been self-serving for the witness to "bend" the facts in this instance, we regard this witness as possibly untrustworthy, and the resulting evidence as suspect.

Circumstantial: The above letter, written by Calvin Hendricks to his sister, also provides an example of *circumstantial*, rather than direct, evidence as to Mrs. Fewens' maiden name. That is, there is no direct statement here that Lona Fewens' maiden name was Hendricks. It is rather something you deduce from the fact that a Calvin Hendricks calls her his sister.

Armed with circumstantial evidence you can sometimes, at least, obtain direct evidence confirming your guess. We will say in this case, for instance, by subsequently searching the marriage records of St. Louis, you find a 1907 marriage license for a William Fewens and a Lona Hendricks, thus providing direct confirming evidence of her maiden name. The same letter also provides circumstantial evidence that Connecticut may have been a prior residence of this Hendricks family. Further research into New Haven records would be needed to substantiate, or overrule, that guess.

When direct, primary sources are lacking, it is necessary to rely upon circumstantial or secondary evidence. Research in those cases requires rigorous analysis and more attention to substantiation by additional sources, to avoid proceeding with false assumptions. An upcoming section will provide helpful guidelines to follow in such cases.

HOW TO JUDGE BETWEEN CONFLICTING FACTS

As a general rule, choose primary over secondary, evidence. For conflicting secondary evidence, choose the one with the more trustworthy source, or made closer to the time of the event, if that information is known. Otherwise, record them both, noting the discrepancy and at that point you'll certainly want to consider what other sources may be consulted to settle the question.

If there are a number of sources with conflicting facts, it often helps to make a discrepancy table in which you list the sources along one side with the facts which came from those sources next to them. Examining the disputed facts in such a format should make it easier for you to make an accurate judgment among those sources. For example, we'll say you have gathered the following sources, with corresponding dates, for an ancestor's birth year:

Source	Birthdate given
death certificate	1876
obituary notice	1878
family Bible (published 1884)	1873
Uncle Ed's memory	1874
1880 census	1872

Fig 4. Example of a Discrepancy Table

The death certificate and obituary notice were all recorded a full lifetime after the birth. Uncle Ed, we shall say, gave you his information even later. Notice the Bible couldn't possibly supply primary evidence because its publication date is more than a decade following the recorded birth date. Apparently, however, it was made closer to the time of birth than all the other sources, except for the 1880 census. This latter source, having been recorded closest to the time of the actual birth date, would appear to be the best secondary evidence we have. Until and unless better evidence is found elsewhere, you should feel satisfied about accepting 1872 as the probable year in which this ancestor was born.

> **When faced with conflicting facts, a discrepencey table will help you jduge which is most likely correct.**

SAFEGUARDS WHEN USING CIRCUMSTANTIAL EVIDENCE

To protect yourself from wrong conclusions when using circumstantial evidence, it is safest to use at least one of the following approaches:

1. *Strengthen your case by getting additional evidence from other sources.*

This is what we did in the above Hendricks-Fewens example when we looked for a marriage license to prove a relationship we had deduced from circumstantial evidence. We might have also looked for the will of Calvin Hendricks' father, in case it included mention of a daughter, Lona; we might also have examined the 1900 New Haven census for all Hendricks families, in case this family was then living there. As you learn about various records, and what kind of data may be found, you'll be expanding your genealogical repertoire; you will then know what sources are appropriate to search for needed additional evidence.

2. *Try to disprove your case.*

This is another good approach. Say, for example, you are looking for the parents of a Robert Wilson, and know he was born in the county of Aberdeen, Scotland. It may be tempting to conclude your search was successful upon finding a christening record for a Robert Wilson in the presumed correct place and time period. This is where many serious genealogical mistakes occur, as an inexperienced researcher might forget to take into account the likelihood of there being (possible many) other contemporary Robert Wilsons who were neighbors to their ancestor.

In order to protect yourself from making this mistake, and thus very possibly picking up the wrong set of ancestors, ask yourself such questions as:

o Could the Robert Wilson found in my research have died young? (You will look through the burial records of this church to find that out.) If he did, he obviously was not your, nor anyone's, ancestor.

o Were there other nearby Wilson families also having children during this time-period? (Besides looking through this parish register to find that out, also check the registers of the nearby parishes, including those of non-conformist churches. You will also want to check other records to learn of candidate Wilson families in the area whose children may not have been baptized.)

By trying to disprove the Robert Wilson originally found in your research as your ancestor, you will often be successful, thereby learning of alternative contemporary Robert Wilsons. Each of these candidate families should then be researched to learn which is the most likely ancestral family. In some cases, however, you will be unsuccessful in finding any other possibilities for alternative candidates, even after careful checking. Only then could you conclude safely that the originally found candidate was probably your ancestor.

DATING ANALYSIS

Are you good at simple mathematics? Although the connection between that field and genealogy might not seem obvious at first, anybody who has worked trying to assemble families from slight data and conflicting dates will soon appreciate it's importance.

> While assembling family data always ask yourself, "Does the chronology make sense?" and then examine it closely to see if it does.

A person born in 1842 is obviously not the same as one who married in 1851, even if the name and place otherwise correspond (except in those Far Eastern countries where marriages between children were arranged by their parents). And a pedigree that shows a mother who has children born to her when she is aged 50 or more will be highly suspect. It is often helpful, if not necessary to estimate dates and ages (for example, in order to know in which time period to conduct your research). The following ideas may help you do this:

o   Knowing the child-bearing years enables you to estimate a mother's age; conversely, knowing the mother's age makes it possible to estimate her children's birthdates. If, for example, the birthdates of her children cover a 20-25 year period, you won't be far wrong in estimating a mother's age as about 20 when her first child was born. An eldest child is generally 20 to 25 years younger than the mother, while the youngest child in a very large family can be much as 40-45 years younger. So knowing birth order, and any facts as to sibling ages again helps you make more accurate estimates.

o   If the child-bearing period of one wife covers much more than 25 years, or if some of the children's birthdates are as close as nine months or less, you'll certainly need to investigate the possibility that births from two different wives or families have been mistakenly intermixed.

o   Local and/or ethnic marriage customs varied. The Irish in Ireland, for example, married noticeably less, and later, than any other European country. Our own reseach has shown that tendency to persist in America at least into the early nineteenth century. 30-40 was more typically the decade for marriages to occur than 20-30. Appalachian brides and grooms, at the other extreme, tended to marry very young, say 13 or 14 in some instances; this has been true even up into this century. From our experience in researching colonial English immigrants and their descendents through several generations, it is rare to find a groom aged much under 18-20, although brides were often as young as 16-17 and, only occasionally, 15. (There is a substantiated case of a bride aged 11 in 1673 Virginia, however; seeming to prove that there are exceptions to all of our genealogical generalities.)

o   Wills often indicate which, if any, of the children are under legal, or perhaps some other, age. (As, for example, "I bequeath to my loving daughter Mary when she reaches age 14. . . . ".) Many other facts found in public or family records provide clues, if not proof, of age. See p. 95 for some of these.

o   Finding a number of children by a prior marriage indicates their parent was older than average at the time of his or her second marriage. And finding a number of grandchildren named in a will further indicates this grandparent was past middle age when writing the will.

o   The average age between generations is about 30 years; where no other clues are forthcoming, you may need to estimate an age or time period using that figure.

As genealogical facts can often be deducted and your genealogical hypotheses either strengthened or disproved through date and age information, chronology obviously must play an important part in your analysis and evaluation. If spotting discrepencies is difficult for you, then consult with someone who can point these out to you. This is necessary at the very least to make sure you haven't misused circumstantial evidence in a way to connect people or generations wrongly. See also Appendix C, if you'll be doing British or American research in the 18th century or earlier, to avoid possible dating mistakes in that era. For each country and time-period you research, investigate the possibility of any other such calendar problems.

SUMMARY

Are you beginning to feel like Sherlock-Holmes' abilities are needed to become a good genealogist? True, sound analytical-deductive work is oftimes required. This is especially so where direct, primary sources are lacking, and you must use circumstantial evidence, or judgment among various secondary sources.

If such detective work isn't, or doesn't become, a strong point, you will be wise to work with somebody who can supply this talent (or who can, at the very least, play "devil's advocate," as you formulate your hypotheses). It likewise helps to engage a patient relative or friend as your sounding-board. Listening to yourself thinking out-loud is sometimes helpful in working your way through a difficult family-tree problem. Or the responses of an objective listener may also provide a different, needed, perspective.

It is far more satisfying for all concerned to pass on a small, but well-substantiated, foundation, on which succeeding generations may build with confidence, than to pass on an inaccurate pedigree, no matter how large.

> **You can't go far wrong if you make it your goal to support your conclusions with evidence that would be upheld even in a court of law. . . . Following such cautions will actually simplify your search by eliminating much or all of the errors that otherwise so easily result.**

This means using direct and primary evidence whenever that is available. If it is not, then your conclusions must be supported by secondary and circumstantial evidence taken from every available source. Even then, it is advisable to couch all such conclusions in tentative terms; e.g.: "It *appears* from these sources. . ." or "thus, it *may* be. . . ." Taking such precautions to assure accuracy may seem difficult or tedious to a beginner, yet following such cautions will actually simplify your search by eliminating much or all of the errors that otherwise so easily result. Don't be satisfied with anything less.

By setting such high standards of veracity, by assidious search into all available records, and especially by careful analysis, in which curious attention ("what might this signify?") is paid to each clue and detail as it turns up, your success becomes ever more guaranteed. For further discussion of evidence, with examples of pitfalls into which an unwary researcher may fall, you may want to consult one or more of these sources:

o Stevenson, Noel C. *Genealogical Evidence. A Guide to the Standard of Proof Relating to Pedigrees, Ancestry, Heirship, and Family History.* Laguna Hills, CA: Aegean Press, 1979.

o National Society of the Daughters of the American Revolution. *Is that Lineage Right?* Washington DC. 1982.

o Harland, Derek. *Genealogical Research Standards.* Salt Lake City, UT: Bookcraft, Inc., 1970.

o Stratton, Eugene. *The Validity of Genealogical Evidence,* in the *National Genealogical Quarterly,* v. 72, Dec., 1984.

Chapter 9. FORMULATING YOUR RESEARCH PLAN

FACTS NEEDED

After you have chosen a line to work on, you must now assemble these specifics to formulate a workable research plan: (1) names; (2) last known exact location; and (3) the time period resided there. If family records reveal this data, use it as the base of your research plan, and skip the following section of examples. But often, only names were passed down. Then you must look for clues to yield the accompanying date and place facts, as in the following examples:

EXAMPLES: LEARNING SPECIFIC PLACES/TIMES

Knowing your ancestor served 4 years as a Confederate soldier allows you deduce a general age and location. As the war went from 1860 to 1864, and assuming he was at least 14 to enlist (Confederate and Revolutionary soldiers including the widest age-span in USA wars) we can figure he was born no later than 1850 (found by subtracting 14 from 1864). But then in interviewing relatives, we'll say you learn his youngest son (your great-grandfather) was born 1871, the same year as his eldest grandchild was born. These facts allow you to move the probable birthdate back two decades; to have a grandchild born 1871, he was most likely born by 1831 (deduced by subtracting an average minimum marriage age of 20, twice, from 1871).

In family interviews you also learn the family's residence was thought to be Kentucky. This again may aid your research, as there is an 1880 census index for families with children under age 10. If your family was still in Kentucky in 1880, you can precisely locate them through that index; as well as learn data such as names, ages, relationships of all living at home, and alleged state of birth of each person's parents. Even if Kentucky was not their residence, you may still be able to locate this family using the 1880 census index, assuming you have the family names to look for, and are willing to search through the indexes of additional southern states (those neighboring Kentucky being the most likely). Depending upon how common their surname was, this could be a tedious search.

When the census indexes are complete for the 1860, 1870, and 1880 censuses, finding this family's location should then be quite easy, even if they had no children under age 10 in 1880, even if the tradition about Kentucky was incorrect, or if *no* family tradition was known. This illustrates the help the AIS or other indexes do or will provide for 19th century American families of unknown residence.

On another line you may learn your grandmother, an eldest child, was born in New York about 1909, shortly after her parent's immigrated from Germany. Thus you look for clues revealing a more specific residence, as New York doesn't yet have an index to its 1910 census. Let's say you find a family picture taken of your great-grandparents' wedding with the name and address of a New York City studio. Maps now allow you to find the specific borough in New York City where this family lived in 1910. And searching that census yields names, ages, and relationships of all family members at home; language spoken, if not English[1]; year of immigration; and if the father was naturalized.

---

[1]Languages are precisely listed; most imply, if not directly give, country of origin (e.g., *Danish* or *Dutch*). And dialects (e.g., *Basque* or *Breton*) may give regional clues.

This data will be quite helpful. As a later chapter explains, you can obtain photocopies of naturalizations since September, 1906. These contain much good information (including, e,g., last foreign address). You will thus follow up clues re: naturalization to gain these records. The less common the name, the more identifying data you can provide about him, his wife and children, and the closer you can approximate when he applyied for naturalization (they will search a five year period), the more likely your success.

On another line, while interviewing and corresponding with family members, a relative shares the photocopy of your grandmother's obituary notice in 1922, giving her age at death as 52, and her place of death.   You then send to that state for her death certificate which gives both her maiden name, Higglesworth, and place of birth, Warwickshire, England. You approximate her birth date by subtracting age at death from date of death, i.e., 1922 minus 52, or 1870. And you then write St. Catherine's House (address in Chapter 15), the repository for English national vital records going back to 1837, for her birth certificate. This provides parent's (including mother's maiden) names, father's occupation, birth date and place, and informant's name; thus allowing you to research back earlier generations. (Note this procedure might not work so well for a very common name. More identification, such as exact birth day, would certainly be necessary to determine which of many *Mary Smiths* born within this approximated time period, is yours.)

If you are in the predicament of not yet knowing the necessary specific time periods and places in which to conduct your research; you will need to do as in the above examples, and follow these steps: (1) consult all possible family sources, looking for pertinent clues, and (2) check finding tools to learn exact residence.

Finding tools are usually indexes that cover large areas (such as a whole country or state) and allow you to determine the county, or even smaller area, of residence. The AIS and other census indexes provide us finding tools for the USA for the 1790-1850 time period. If your ancestor lived during another time, or abroad, or simply does not show up on the censuses or their indexes, then you will need another finding tool. Fortunately, many such indexes are already available, and a number are being done. Updated guidebooks, to be discussed in our next chapter, may need to be consulted to learn what indexes exist for the general area of interest. Each indexed work, in turn, may need to be consulted until you finally learn your ancestor's specific residence.

Specific names, dates, and places must be known before research can begin.

DEFINING YOUR GOALS

Once you have specific names, places, and times, you next want to define your goals. This is simple. List next to the names of your ancestors the information desired. Let's say you want the birthdates, birthplaces and parents of your grandparents, Cyrus Brown and (his wife) Mary Funk. Those are your goals. Write your goals on the research agenda to keep from being drawn off into obviously unproductive tangents.

To reach these goals, you must analyze what is now known. Begin by writing down a brief, but complete as possible, biography of these ancestors. Leave lots of room to add questions or possible sources to search which may come to mind in reviewing these facts. The following example has parenthetical remarks to illustrate the analytical thinking and planning of an experienced researcher:

EXAMPLE: AN ANALYSIS TO MAKE UP A RESEARCH PLAN

Cyrus Brown was a farmer; his earliest known residence was Hard Rock, Kansas, about 1885. (So there may be Hard Rock land records for him. His earliest deed may even give his prior residence. We will check the county courthouse for these.)

His wife was Mary Funk; her mother's maiden name was Ethel Showalter; and four children are known: Mary, Ellen, Barbara, and George. Barbara married Bill Read in Hard Rock. George, married Anne, her surname and their marriage place unknown. (Other names besides Browns we will look for as we search the county records, then, will be Funks, Showalters, and Reads; variants, such as Reids or Reeds, will be noted as well.)

Cyrus died and the family moved to Colorado by 1898. (There may be probate and perhaps guardian records for Cyrus in Kansas; check for these also at the county courthouse. We'll also check the 1900 Colorado census index to pick up the ages of remaining family members, and to learn the state of birth for Mary Funk.)

The widow of Cyrus remarried, date unknown, to a James Brown; no children by him. (Could he be a relation to Cyrus? Maybe we will find further facts on him as we gather Brown data from our Kansas courthouse. We will want to look for this family under the names of both James and Mary Brown on the 1900 Colorado census, as we don't yet know if they were married by this date.

We will also look for the married daughter, Barbara, under the name of her husband, William or Bill Read, on both the Kansas and Colorado census indexes. Because she married in Hard Rock, rather than in Colorado, that marriage probably occurred before the family left there in 1898, so she was probably born by about 1880. Learning her birthday and place, given on the 1900 census, will thus help us determine the likely state in which Cyrus and Mary were living in 1880.

Once located on the 1880 census, we will not only have the place and approximate time of birth for Cyrus [data already obtained for Mary on the 1900 Colorado census], but we will than also know the reported state of birth for the parents of both he and Mary.)

(The 1910 Colorado census would also be worth searching, but as no index currently exists for it, we could only find them easily if they happen to still be living in the same place as on the 1900 census. We will therefore make note of their exact (township, and/or street) location when we find them on the 1900 census. If James or Mary are still living in 1910, that census will give us their number of years married, and number of previous marriages. Knowing the marriage year will help us know where, as well as when, to search for their marriage certificate. This latter may again supply facts about Mary Funk's origin, and perhaps, indirectly, something about Cyrus' origin, if he is related to James.

And if the census showed, for instance, this to be a third marriage for Mary, we would suspect she married once prior to Cyrus, and Funk might have been her first married name, rather than her maiden name. Having reason to suspect such a possibility would, of course, importantly affect our research strategy.)

The Browns were known to be Lutherans. (Excellent. We can send off a letter to the Hard Rock Lutheran Church asking them what church records are extant for that time period and how we may use them. Or, alternatively, we can look up that denomination in *The Source*, e.g., where we learn that 95% of American Lutheran Churches are listed by synod in the *Lutheran Church Directory for the United States*, and extensive microfilming of these records has begun. Further, as there is a microfiche catalog to those microfilmed records, we can use it to quickly learn whether the records of our Hard Rock congregation are included.

Because Lutheran church records are among the best, genealogically, we will definitely want to track down these records for our Browns.)

> The family facts you've gathered can now lead you to public records containing even more data.

Of course, the above suggestions would not be obvious to a beginner. Before you could confidently draw up such an effective plan, you must first learn what record sources there are in the place and time you wish to search, and what may be contained therein. The chapters to follow will help you gain that knowledge; and certainly your skills will increase even more with actual researching experience.

For now, write up a biography, as complete as possible, of the person(s) you want to research, including as many of the following facts as you can learn: approximated or known *ages*, known to be in which *places* when; *social status* (note amount of property owned from land or census records, as well as titles of respect in early time periods); *ethnic and/or religious background*, and *names of* children, spouse(s), siblings, parents, or any other known or suspected *relatives*. Go back to these facts often; as your researching experience grows, your ability to effectively utilize them to plan productive research will grow correspondingly.

Of course, analysis of your facts has to be an on-going procedure. You use it not only prior to making up your research plan, as just illustrated, but each time you obtain new data. We'll say, for example, that searching the 1900 census gives you Barbara (Brown) Read's birth as 1879 in Missouri; and her brother's as 1881, also in Missouri. You then go to the indexed 1880 Missouri census, and, in locating this family, learn that Cyrus Brown was born about 1850, in Virginia, as were his parents, and Mary Funk was born about 1855, in Pennsylvania, as were her parents. Your goals have been realized.

These facts also open new possibilities; maybe you now want to learn about the grandparents of Cyrus and Mary. If so, you need to familiarize yourself with mid-19th century USA, Pennsylvania, Virginia, and Missouri sources, even as you previously needed to learn about USA, Kansas, and Colorado sources of a slightly later time period.

> To help your data analysis: (1) Keep your research summary sheet current to ensure thinking through and writing down research results. (2) Occasionally discuss your progress (or lack of) with one more experienced than you.

SUMMARY

Add to your research agenda, the specific facts for which you are looking, i.e. *your goals*. If you don't yet know the specific county or town location of your ancestors, than you now need to use indexes, or other finding aids, to obtain that information. Besides the ancestral facts recorded in chart form, it's additionally helpful to write up a short biography of those you've chosen to research, and to analyze those facts regularly throughout your search. You will next learn how to find out what sources are available for a given place and time period, and other necessary background.

Chapter 10. GEOGRAPHY, HISTORY & JURISDICTIONS

GEOGRAPHY

Finding Location: You must know your ancestor's exact location (generally county for USA, town or parish for Europe and New England) so you can locate their records. If your folks came from Hard Rock, you now need to precisely locate that town on a Kansas map to learn in which county it was located. If family records state the immigrant birthplace as Eastersnow, Ireland, you now need to determine what it was (parish, town or townland, province, barony, diocese, or county) and just where in Ireland it was located.

If the country's boundaries and place names have remained relatively stable, then geographical background may be obtained by simply looking up the place name on a current map. But many have not; then additional searching (e.g., of more detailed road maps, postal guides, shipping almanacs, or gazetteers) will be needed. If still unsuccessful, it may no longer exist; earlier maps and historical gazetteers must then be examined. Consult the sources listed in this chapter's bibliography first; and then, if need be, with a librariarn or other expert, so as to not overlook any important source.

When wanting to trace a Scottish line some years ago, we first examined family data in this country. We thereby learned our immigrant ancestor once wrote his birthplace as *Kinner* and once as *Larbor*, while his wife always gave hers as *Alloa*. We then began our geographical search in a nearby university library that had a good worldwide map and gazetteer collection. In the excellent source, Lewis' *Topographical Dictionary* (see Bibliography) we found listings for the small mining town of Kinnaird, located in Larbert Parish, Sterlingshire, adjacent to tiny Clackmannanshire, which included the town of Alloa.

Having thus precisely located their birthplaces, we could then take advantage of the excellent Scottish collection of the GSU accessible through their *Locality Catalog*. Primarily through microfilmed census and parish records, we added three generations of Scottish forebears to our pedigree. We could not have done this, of course, without fulfilling this ever-necessary preliminary of exact place-location.

Placename Considerations: As in the above example, expect to find some differences between the current spelling of the place name, and spellings obtained from family or other records. This means, of course, looking for possible spelling variations in your geographical search. Just as importantly, it implies the need to first search out all instances where your ancestor referred to his birthplace.

Be thorough here, as family traditions about the immigrant's birthplace are often in error. If they came from a town with a long or difficult name, the tendency was to mistakenly pass down an easier, or at least a more familiar name (maybe mentioned by the ancestor at one time) as the place of origin. And for some immigrants who earned their passage money in a port city prior to departure, that port city haa been mistakenly passed down as the birthplace. (Thus Liverpool, Cork, or Hamburg, for example, should probably be considered suspect as a birthplace until corroboration is found.) Further research may also be needed to determine whether a placename such as Wicklow, Ireland, refers to the county, city, or town, of that same name.

> **Thoroughly search out records about your immigrant in this country, because family traditions about the immigrant's birthplace are often wrong.**

Boundary Changes: Even when exact residence in learned, further geographical background may be needed to take boundary changes into account. The USA, a relatively new and fast-growing country, has had numerous such changes going back to its earliest history; the colonies themselves went through long periods of boundary disputes. (As one extreme example, we found pertinent sources for an area in present day Delaware among colonial Pennsylvania, Maryland and, even, New York records!)

Several other countries, exemplified by the old Austro-Hungarian and German Empires have suffered extensive, complicated and dramatic boundary shifts, as a result of wars and constant political change. Some GSU *Research Papers* give specifics and maps that will help the genealogists working in these areas, including many modern Communist countries. *Genealogy Unlimited, Inc.* (789 So. Buffalo Grove Rd, IL 60089) advertises they can locate "most towns in 1871-1918 German Empire." They charge $2.50 per town-name search. *Jonathan Sheppard Books* (address in Chapter 15) has over over 200 worldwide maps in their collection; these are described in a catalog that costs $1 and is refundable.

Even countries of relatively stable history have been subject to boundary changes. In England, for instance, several counties disappeared or were renamed in 1950. In tracing boundary changes, seek to learn the dates and specific places involved. In the case of the USA, for instance, the records of the original county almost always remained there when an offshoot county was formed. So even if your family didn't move, but if they lived in a break-off area, you may expect to find their records in at least the two counties involved (and more, if they lived in and during additional county break-offs).

Besides the LDSGL *Research Papers* which provide boundary changes for several countries, there are also reference books to help you trace past USA boundary changes (the first two of these are not complete about some now-defunct counties; the last excellent source will be mentioned later on):

-Jackson, Ronald V., and Teeples, Gary R. *Encyclopedia of Local History and Genealogy. U.S. Counties.* Bountiful, UT: Accelerated Indexing Systems, 1977.

-Everton, George B., ed. *The Handy Book for Genealogists*, seventh edition, Logan, UT: Everton Publishers, Inc. 4th pr., 1984. (has geography for other countries also.)

-Thorndale, William, and Dollarhide, William. *Map Guide to the U.S. Federal Censuses 1790-1920.* Baltimore, MD: Genealogical Publishing, 1987.

Topographical Considerations: Having learned that Hard Rock was in Sassafrass Co. when your Cyrus Brown family lived there, you would generally expect to find their civil records in that county seat. By checking a topographical map, however, you may find that intervening between Hard Rock and its own county seat town is a rugged, hilly area; further, Hard Rock, being in the perimeter of the county, is closer to an adjacent county seat than to its own. So if a search of the Sassafrass County records doesn't yield the Brown data anticipated, you will know to expand your search to include the adjacent county seat.

Because a topographical map does show the physical lie of the land, it's useful in ways besides helping you spot such likely boundary problems. A topographical map of a large area, for instance, will also help you figure likely migration routes used by your ancestors, inasmuch as these developed in accordance with natural surroundings, and generally followed the lines of least resistance.

Topographical maps can suggest the family's migration pattern or help you track down their records in case of boundary problems.

Obtaining Good Map & Atlas Sources: Maps, then, helping us as they do to visualize and understand such important background, are an important source to examine early in your research project. Study and make photocopies of appropriate maps, especially those contemporary with the time period of your interest. A major research library specializing in your area of interest is usually the best place to find these. Sources listed in our Bibliography should also provide good help. And local genealogical and historical societies, if not themselves a good source for obtaining helpful area maps, can often direct you to these.

The excellent, brand-new source for American reserchers mentioned above (*Map Guide to the U.S. Federal Censuses 1790-1920*, by Thorndale and Dollarhide) contains the first complete set of maps showing the evolution of the USA county boundaries. It also has a wealth of information concerning the early federal censuses to help the researcher, and a most helpful bibliography. Close to 400 individual state maps are included. It will be available summer, 1987, and should prove to be a real boon to all researching in this country.

Sometimes you'll even find genealogical data in with geographical information. We were greatly aided, for instance, while doing early NY research, by a most helpful 1860 Gazetteer. It not only included much helpful historical and geographical data, but even gave the names of the earliest settlers. And for one town of our interest, it named the town in Connecticut from whence these original New York settlers emigrated, allowing us to greatly extend our research. Look also for the evidence provided by many early land-ownership maps that have the landowner names inscribed inside their property boundaries.

HISTORY

After you have attended to this important matter of geography, read the local and regional histories of the area. Use library card catalogs, including the GSU *Locality Catalog*, and good bibliographies, to learn of the important historical works. As you become familiar with the historical background, you will probably notice how isolated facts you have so far been collecting will begin to "fit" (analogous to how seeing the completed picture of a jigsaw puzzle helps you then better sort out and put the individual pieces together).

LEARNING ABOUT RECORDS THROUGH LOCAL RESEARCH GUIDES

Once familiar with the geography and history, learn practical specifics regarding sources and records: i.e., what is available, where can they be found, and what facts might be found in them. Based on this information, you can finish making up an effective and realistic research plan by writing these upon your research agenda, and then searching carefully through them. In recent years a number of good-to-excellent books, pamphlets, and guides have been written on how to research particular countries, regions, states and counties; they generally supply this needed information. All USA researchers, for instance, will want to utilize Eakle and Cerni's *The Source*, an excellent and comprehensive guidebook that should be at your local library. This, with other helpful books for the USA and various countries, are listed at the end of this chapter. Also look for those covering the more specific desired locales.

Our own research, for example, has been recently benefitted by this small, but helpful, guide: *Virginia Genealogical Research* by George K. Schweitzer. (Knoxville, TN, 1982.) (Schweitzer, address in Chapter 15, has also written good guide books for the following: Kentucky, North Carolina, Pennsylvania, South Carolina, Tennessee, the Revoluation War, the War of 1812, the Civil War, and a general guide. We have additionally been quite impressed with the depth shown in the following source book: *North Carolina Research: Genealogy and Local History* by Helen F. M. Leary and Maurice R. Stirewalt, eds. (Raleigh, NC: North Carolina Genealogical Society, 1980.)

These works are exemplary of numerous other such guides, large and small, now available for various states and counties; look for these during your library research. As previously-mentioned, the GSU has a number of good *research papers* for many countries, and *outlines* available for each of the 50 United States. These latter papers are brief (1-8 pages in length), so you would certainly need to supplement them with more in-depth texts. However, they provide a good starting point for beginners, and the price is right (i.e., free with an SASE). And those unsuccessful in locating a good and up-to-date *How to Research in. . . .(your area of interest)* book, may want to write the appropriate local historical or genealogical societies for their suggestions here.

> **There are good to excellent guidebooks covering most areas; these help you plan effective research.**

JURISDICTIONS

Definition and Importance: The various facts you now seek are the result of record-keeping by various spheres of authority, or *jurisdictions*, as we shall here refer to them. Your ancestors may well have been involved with several jurisdictions concurrently. Certainly they were residents, if not citizens, so various governmental agencies in their country had legal authority to make various records on their behalf. Censuses, probates, naturalizations, and land sales are some of these; all may be of value. As family members, your ancestors were likewise part of another jurisdiction that may have taken upon itself responsibility for making and keeping (family) records. And churches, schools, fraternities, businesses; hospitals, and prisons were other organizations which again often assumed the authority to make various records on behalf of their members. (*The Source* provides good information on using several of these less commonly used record sources for American researchers.)

Sometimes Need to Search Many: Some may be quickly successful in obtaining good records kept by family and governmental jurisdictions (such as family Bibles, vital certificates, wills, land records, or censuses). If so, there may be no need to search out additional jurisdictions for your ancestor. But others whose family and governmental records are missing, or deficient, will need to do this.

As an example of the siginificant help one jurisdiction may provide, we offer our nineteenth-century Irish-Canadian ancestry. Little family facts had been passed down; and, because they were mostly illiterate and poor, few land and probate records resulted. They had the very common Irish names of Sullivan and McCormick. Additionally, Canadians are difficult to locate on censuses as these are as yet unindexed. So they would have been poor researching prospects except for one important advantage: they were Catholics.

The Catholic church generally kept very good records. Even marginally active members at least used the local priests to marry them and christen their children, and so are found in the parish records. And the Catholic priests we have written have generally responded well. (When requesting such help, we include a small check of $5.00 or so, as slight renumeration for the time and effort required to search out and send two or three complete record entries.)

Necessary Background: Of course, knowing some of our ancestors were Catholic did not help our research until we learned *what* kind of Catholic records there were, *where* they were, and *how* we could obtain them. This is background you may also need, unless the records of your interest have already been microfilmed--as many have. Perhaps by now you have learned to what extent you may rely upon microfilms by examining our old friend, the *Locality Catalog*. If microfilming by the GSU is incomplete, however, then you must likewise learn these *whats, wheres*, and *hows*, to obtain desired records.

These kinds of facts are often found in the guidebooks and other researching aids you will now seek to obtain. The address sources found in Chapter 15 may also help. And in the few remaining cases where not otherwise available, you will need to consult with experts as recommended by the appropriate genealogical or historical society to gain this background.

In our case, because some of the pertinent Catholic church records were recently microfilmed, along with Canadian governmental records, this has definitely helped our current Irish-Canadian research. We can now progress faster and more efficiently than when we could only proceed one letter and one priest or government official at a time.

Which Sources to Search: Because direct, primary evidence is preferred, therefore the most important jurisdictions, and the ones you'll want to look in first, will be those producing vital records. How to find and use these will thus begin our discussion of records found in upcoming chapters. Probably most will find that diligent searching in the record groups covered in the next three chapters is sufficient to obtain desired family facts. However, we have concentrated on sources that have proven most helpful for USA research (with some overlap for Anglos, and Western Europeans).

For other countries and ethnic groups you may also need to consider sources besides, or instead of, these. And, because no family is at a dead-end until every possible pertinent record has been exhaustively searched, therefore, even some British-American families may require your extending the scope of search beyond these covered sources. If necessary, learn what additional sources exist through a research paper, guidebook, or by consulting a genealogical expert for the area.

No family can be considered at a dead-end until every possibly pertinent record has been searched.

SUMMARY:

You need specific background about the geography, history, jurisdictions, and records for your chosen area of research. We advise you not to shortcut here. You will usually obtain this background most efficiently through study of the guidebooks or research papers dealing with your area of interest. The following Bibliography provides several other helpful aids.

BIBLIOGRAPHY: 1. GEOGRAPHICAL TOOLS

Adams, James T., and Jackson, Kenneth T. *Atlas of American History*. Rev. ed. NY: Scribner's, 1978.

American Geographic Society. *Index to Maps in Books and Periodicals*. 10 vols. Boston, MA: G K Hall, 1971; 2 vol. Supplement, 1976.

Bennett, James D. *Post Offices in the United States in 1890*. Ingleside, TX, 1973. A postal history gazetteer.

The Columbia Lippincott Gazetteer of the World. NY: Columbia Univ. Press, 1962.

Cram's Family Atlas of the World. 64th ed. Indianapolis, IN, 1952.

Davenport, Bishop. *A New Gazetteer, or Geographical Dictionary of North America and the West Indies*. . .Phil, PA, 1838, etc.

Rand McNally and Co. *Commercial Atlas and Marketing Guide*. Chicago: 67th ed. 1936. Annual.

Andriot, John L., comp. *Township Atlas of the United States: Named Townships*. McLean, Virginia: Andriot Associates, 1977.

Cappon, Lester J., et al. *Atlas of Early American History: the Revolutionary Era, 1760-1790*. Princeton, NJ: Princeton University Press, 1976.

Carrington, David K, and Stephenson, Richard W., *Map Collections in the United States and Canada: a Directory*. 3rd ed. NY: Special Libraries Association, 1978.

Department of the Interior. *Catalog of the United States Geological Survey Library*. 25 vols. Boston, MA: G K Hall, 1964; 15 vol. Supplement, 1972-4.

Hargett, Janet L. *List of Selected Maps of States and Territories*. repr. Washington, DC: National Archives, 1976.

Hayward, John. *A Gazetteer of the United States*. repr. Knightstown, IN: Bookmark, 1977.

Jackson, Richard H., *Historical and Genealogical Atlas of North America: Volume 1. United States East of the Mississippi*. Provo, UT: Gentech, 1974.

Kirkham, E. Kay. *A Genealogical and Historical Atlas of the United States of America*. 2nd ed. Logan, UT: Everton, 1980.

LeGear, Clara Egli. *United States Atlases; a List of National, State, County, City, and Regional Atlases in the Library of Congress*. 2 vol. Wash., DC: L.C, 1950-3.

Lewis, Samuel A. *A Topographical Dictionary of England*. 1831, 1833, et al. London, or available in microfiche. SLC, UT: Traditions Pub., 1977. Indispensable source.

Library of Congress. *The Bibliography of Cartography*. 5 vols., Boston, MA: G K Hall, 1973; 2 vol. Supplement, 1979.

Paullin, Charles O, and Wright, John K. *Atlas of the Historical Geography of the United States*. repr. Westport, CT: Greenwood PR., 1975.

Sale, Randall D., and Karn, Edwin D. *American Expansion: a Book of Maps*. (A map for each census year 1790-1900)

The Phillimore Atlas and Index of Parish Registers. Humphery Smith, Cecil, ed., Baltimore, MD: Genealogical Publishing Co., 1984. Good.

Sealock, Richard B., and Seely, Pauline A. *Bibliography of Place Name Literature, U.S. and Canada*. 3rd ed. Chicago: American Library Association, 1982. (Updated by supplementary lists in the periodical entitled *Names*.)

"A Selected Bibliography of Statewide Place Name Literature, Old Gazetteers, Postal Service Histories, Ghost Town Directories and Histories, and Boundary Change Guides" in *Library Service for Genealogists*, pp 2947. J. Carlyle Parker, ed. Gale Genealogy and Local History Series, Vol. 15. Detroit: Gale Research Co., 1981.

Vallentine, John F. *Locality Finding Aids for U.S. Surnames*. 2nd ed. Logan, UT: Everton, 1981.

2. GUIDES FOR A NUMBER OF COUNTRIES

Schweitzer, George K. *Genealogical Source Handbook*. Knoxville, TN: The Author. 1982. Brief lists of recommended materials for many countries, ethnic groups & research categories.

The GSU (See Chapter 2) provides research papers for numerous countries.

Beard, T.F. *How to Find Your Family Roots*. McGrawHill, NYC, NY: 1977. Good detailed sections on many countries and ethnic groups.

Baxter, Angus. *In Search of Your European Roots*. Baltimore: Genealogical Pub. Co., 1985. Covers every European country.

3. ETHNIC AND NATIONAL GUIDEBOOKS

Eakle, Arlene and Cerny, Johni, eds. *The Source: A Guidebook of American Genealogy*. Salt Lake City, UT: Ancestry Pub., 1984. A massive, excellent survey.

Bremer, R.A.. *Compendium of Historical Sources: The How and Where of American Genealogy* Salt Lake City, UT: Butterfly Publishing. 1984. 1,000+ pp.

Rubincam, Milton, ed. *Genealogical Research: Methods and Sources*. GOOD. Vol 1: Eastern seaboard states; Canada; Europe. Vol. 2: Central USA, Florida, Ontario, Huguenot, Jewish & Black. Washington, DC: American Society of Genealogists, 1980-3.

Stevenson, Noel C. *Search and Research: The Researchers Handbook. a Guide to Offical Records and Library Sources for Investigators, Historians, Genealogists, Lawyers, and Librarians*. Salt Lake City UT: Deseret Book Co. Rev.ed., 1977.

Greenwood, Val D. *The Researcher's Guide to American Genealogy*. Baltimore, MD: Gen. Pub. Co., Revised ed., 1987. A classic work; we're look forward to this new edition.

Virkus, Frederick A., *Compendium of American Genealogy*. Baltimore: Gen. Pub. Co. 7 vols; reissue, 1987. Errors, but still helpful for early, especially prominent, families.

Crandall, Ralph J., ed. *Genealogical Research in New England*. Genealogical Publishing Co.: Baltimore, MD: 1984. Complete guide to research in the six New England states.

Torrey, Clarence A. *New England Marriages Prior to 1700*. Gen. Pub. Co.: Baltimore, MD. 1985. Names of virtually every married couple living in 17th century New England.

Senekovic, Dagmar. *Handy Guide to Austrian Genealogical Sources*. Logan, UT: The Everton Publishers, Inc., 1979.

Jonasson, Eric. *The Canadian Genealogical Handbook: a Comprehensive Guide to Finding Your Ancestors in Canada*, 3rd ed., Winnipeg: Wheatfield Pr, 1983.

Baxter, Angus. *In Search of Your Roots: A Guide for Canadians Seeking their Ancestry*. Baltimore, MD: Gen. Pub. Co., Rev & updated, 1984.

Franklin, Charles M. *Dutch Genealogical Research*. Indianapolis, IN: Heritage House, 1982.

Gardner, David E., and Smith, Frank. *Genealogical Research in England and Wales*. 3 vols. Salt Lake City: Bookcraft, 1964-1966.

Smith, Frank. *Genealogical Gazetteer of England*. Baltimore: Gen. Pub. Co., 4th pr., 1982.

Hamilton-Edwards, Gerald K. Savery. *In Search of British Ancestry*. 4th ed. Baltimore: Gen. Pub. Co., 1983.

_____. *In Search of Scottish Ancestry*. 2nd ed. Baltimore: Gen. Pub. Co., 1984.

Falley, Margaret D. *Irish and Scotch-Irish Ancestral Research: a Guide to the Genealogical Records, Methods and Sources in Ireland*. 2 vols. Baltimore: Gen. Pub. Co.; repr., 1984.

Bloxham, V. Ben, comp. *Key to the Parochial Registers of Scotland From Earliest Times Through 1854*. Provo: Brigham Young University Press, 1970.

Rose, James M. and Eichholz, Alice, eds. *Black Genesis*. Gale Genealogy Local History Series, Vol. 1. Detroit: Gale Research Co., 1976. (A bibliographic guide.)

Walker, James D. *Black Genealogy: How to Begin*. Athens, GA: The Univ. Press, 1977.

Miller, Olga, ed. *Genealogical Research for Czech and Slovak Americans*. Gale Genealogy & Local History Series, Vol. 2. Detroit: Gale Research Co., 1978.

Kirkham, E. Kay, comp. *Our Native Americans and Their Records of Genealogical Value*. 2 vols., Logan, UT: Everton Publishers, 19804.

Kurzweil, Arthur. *From Generation to Generation: How to Trace Your Jewish Genealogy and Personal History*. Wm. Morrow & Co., Inc. NY: 1980.

Rottenberg, Dan. *Finding Our Fathers: A Guidebook to Jewish Genealogy*. Baltimore: Gen. Pub. Co., 1986.

Jensen, Larry O. *Genealogical Handbook of German Research*. Pleasant Grove, UT: The Author, 1980-3. 2 Vol. Sold by Everton. Good.

Smith, Clifford Neal & Anna P. *Encyclopedia of German-American Genealogical Research*. NY: R R Bowker, 1976.

_____. *American Genealogical Resources in German Archives: a Handbook*. Munich: Verlag Dokumentation; NY: R R Bowker, 1977.

Platt, Lyman D., ed. *Genealogical-Historical Guide to Latin America*. Gale Genealogy Local History Series, vol. 4. Detroit: Gale Research Co., 1978.

Johansson, Carl-Erik. *Cradled in Sweden*. Rev. ed. Logan, UT: Everton, 1980.

Suess, Jared H. *Handy Guide to Swiss Genealogical Records*. Logan, UT: Everton, 1980.

Nielson, Paul A. *Swiss Genealogical Research: An Introductory Guide*. Norfolk, VA: Donning, 1979.

Smith, Jessie C., ed. *Ethnic Genealogy: A Research Guide*. Westport, CT: Greenwood Press, 1983. (Native, Asian, Hispanic and Black American records and research.)

Ryskamp, George R. *Tracing Your Hispanic Heritage*. The Author, 1985. Guide to Spanish, Mexican, and Latin-American records.

Chapter 11. VITAL RECORDS: GOVERNMENT, CHURCH, CEMETERY

When well prepared for, and thoroughly carried out, searching in *original records* usually provides your most exciting and productive research. These were the records made during and soon after your ancestor's lifetimes. Some you'll want to examine are listed below step #6B on our Research Procedure Diagram (Appendix A), and will now be covered.

As pointed out earlier, your first hope is that *vital records* were made and are still available. These records were made at the time of a person's milestone events: birth, marriage, and death. They may also include records of closely associated events, such as christenings (in most churches took place in infancy, soon after the child's birth), burials, and notices of banns, engagements, or marriage bonds. (These latter pre-maritial records provide only circumstantial evidence of a marriage, however; unless the marriage date was initialed on afterwards, as was common for marriage bonds.) We substitute associated event records, of course, only if records of the actual events aren't available. The recording of vital facts may have been done by any of several jurisdictions. As we have already talked about family records, the most common source of vital statistics, this chapter therefore concentrates on other principal sources: government, church, and cemetery.

> We look for Vital Records, with their valuable direct, primary evidence, first.

GOVERNMENT VITAL RECORDS

United States vital records are of relatively recent origin, and in that respect weak when compared to many other countries. Nevertheless, they are most helpful when in existence, and so should be routinely searched for each family member. Generally you'll want to do this after a thorough examination of family sources, and before looking for any other record. The first jurisdiction to check for vital registration in the United States, is the state. On the next page is a list of the dates when each state began their vital registration, or from when the majority of records occur. *c.l.o., *county level only*, i.e., no state records; ** if records began at a different (usually earlier) time for at least one large city within that state; and @ if some earlier records or abstracts exist. Not shown on the chart, New Jersey's vital records between May 1848 and May 1878 are in her State Archives, and Vermont has a nearly complete index to all her vital records.

You can obtain vital registration certificates from the respective Departments of Health or Vital Statistics found in each state capitol. The costs vary from state to state and may change frequently. To obtain updated price and address information for any state, simply call your local Department of Health. This information is also in *Where to Write for Vital Records: Births, Deaths, Marriages, and Divorces*, put out by the U.S. Dept of Health & Human Services; and also provides specifics about any city records different from the rest of the state (e.g., New Orleans began keeping birth records in 1790, while the rest of Louisiana didn't require them until 1914!)

When ordering a vital certificate, give as specific name, date, place and parent data as you have. Include your relationship and purpose (*family research* is acceptable). As seen from this chart, required state registration has been relatively recent for most states. Fortunately, however, counties (and towns in New England) often recorded their births, marriages, and deaths long before the states. In some cases these go back to date of creation, although with usually less complete coverage than when later required by state legislation. So

state	birth; death records	marriage; divorce records
AL	Jan 1908	Aug 1936 , M; Jan 1950 , Di
AK	1913	1913 M; 1950 Di
AZ	July 1909 @	*c.l.o.
AR	Feb 1914	1917 M; 1923 M
CA	July 1905	July 1905 M; *c.l.o. Di
CO	1910 B; 1910 De	no marr recs 1940–67
CT	July 1897	July 1897 M; index only , 1947 Di
DE	1861–3 , 1881+	1847 M; 1935 Di
FL	Jan 1917 @	6 June 1927
GA	Jan 1919	9 June 1952
HI	1853	1853 M; July 1951 Di
ID	1911	Jan 1947
IL	Jan 1916	Jan 1962
IN	Oct 1907 B; 1900 De	index only , 1958 M; *c.l.o. Di
IA	July 1880	July 1880 M; brief data only , 1906 Di
KS	July 1911	May 1913 M; July 1951 Di
KY	Jan 1911	June 1958
LA	July 1914 **	*c.l.o.
ME	1892	Jan 1892
MD	Aug 1898 **	June 1951 M; Jan 1961 Di
MA	1841 **	1841 M; Index only , 1952 Di
MI	1867 **	Apr 1867 M; 1897 Di
MN	Jan 1908	index only , Jan 1958 M; Jan 1970 Di
MS	1912	brief , 1926–Jul 1938 , 1942 M; 1926 Di index
MO	Jan 1910	index only , July 1948
MT	late 1907	July 1943
NB	late 1904	Jan 1909
NV	July 1911	index only , Jan 1968
NH	1640	1640 M; 1808 Di
NJ	June 1878 (& see p. 71)	June 1878 M; Di from State Superior Ct
NM	1920 (@ 1880)	*c.l.o.
NY	1880 **	May 1915 M; Jan 1963 Di
NC	Oct 1913 B; Jan 1930 De	Jan 1962 M , Jan 1958 Di
ND	1920 (@ from 1893)	Jul 1925 M; index only , Jul 1949 Di
OH	20 Dec 1908	Sept 1949
OK	Oct 1908	*c.l.o.
OR	Jan 1903 **	Jan 1906 M; 1925 Di
PA	Jan 1906 **	Jan 1941 M; Jan 1946 Di
RI	1853	Jan 1853 M; Di from State Clk Fam Ct
SC	Jan 1915 **	Jul 1950 M; July 1962
SD	July 1905	July 1905
TN	Jan 1914 **	July 1945
TX	1903	Jan 1966 M; Jan 1968 Di
UT	1905 **	1978
VT	(See p. 71)	
VA	1853–96 , 4 Jun 1912	Jan 1853 M; Jan 1918 Di
WA	Jul 1907	Jan 1968
WV	Jan 1917	Jan 1921 M; index only , 1968 Di
WI	Oct 1907 @	Oct 1907
WY	Jul 1909	May 1941

Fig. 5. Beginning Dates for State Vital Registration

after all available state certificates are obtained, check county or town next.

Most states have assembled their early county, city, or town records, including vital records made before state registration requirements. Thus, a visit to the appropriate State *Archives* is helpful, if not necessary, to examine these. Here in Virginia, for example, the earliest available county records, up to the year 1865, are microfilmed and in the Virginia State Archives; the county itself often doesn't have its own early records. Neighboring North Carolina has even more aggressively gathered early county records into her State Archives; so that a researcher must go to Raleigh to see these.

The GSU has microfilmed many, but by no means all, of these early records in the respective State Archives. Use their *Locality Catalog* to learn which are thus available through the GSU, or (for those lucky enough to be researching their state of residence) check with a librarian to learn if and how you can obtain State Archives sources on loan through a local library.

Your State Archive sources may be loanable through a local library.

The previously cited Everton's *Handy Book* is quite helpful here as it lists all records, including vital, available at the county level. Also check during your library research for published vital records. Where available, and depending upon their accuracy, these usually simplify your research. At the very least they provide a helpful index to the original records so you may then more easily obtain them. The quality of such published works will vary according to the conscientiousness and ability of the compiler. In some cases, as where notes are added by a knowledgable genealogist, they may be even more helpful to you than the originals. Nevertheless, as secondary sources so often contain at least some errors or incomplete reporting of the facts when compared to the original, you'll be wise to additionally examine the original records whenever possible.

As by now you have written appropriate sources of information onto your research agenda, you now want to obtain these. For vital records this will require writing the State office; the county clerk (who may go by another title. Everton's *Handy Book* gives that, and the address); or else ordering the appropriate microfilm. Where you have a choice, we suggest you first use the microfilms for reasons explained in Chapter 15.

CHURCH VITAL RECORDS

Churches often recorded marriages, christenings, and burials, and sometimes recorded births and deaths and other possibly pertinent facts. As with the Irish-Canadian Catholics given previously, church records for at least some groups may be equal or superior to contemporary govenment vital records, and often predate them as well. Other Church groups with usually good records are the New England Congregationalists, the Quakers (this church including a large number of our early colonists), Moravians, German and Dutch Reformed Churches, Lutherans, LDS (*Mormons*), and Episcopalians.

Because of the anti-English attitude consequent to the Revolutionary period, many early official Anglican (later known as Protestant Episcopal) Church records in the Southern colonies were neglected, destroyed, or otherwise disappeared. This has resulted in a lamentable gap for many church-going colonists. No 18th century North Carolina Anglican records are known to be extant, for example, and comparatively few early Virginia parish registers survived. This illustrates how for some church records, your search may be unsuccessful.

Methodist, Baptist and various evangalistic denominations often lack vital records and tend to be difficult to track down. There are wide variations in the record-keeping practices among and between various churches. We therefore recommend some preliminary investigation (*Church Records*, in *The Source*, provides this data for the main USA denominations) to give you an idea of the amount of effort needed to obtain those records. If a tedious search seems indicated, or if your ancestor's denomination was notorious for poor record-keeping, you may well prefer to first search for court, land, and census records.

> **Church records can be excellent or disappointingly sparse. The difference depended at least as much upon the denominational record—keeping traditions as upon how conscientious the individual minister was.**

There are two prerequisites for using church records:

o *determining with which church your ancestral family was associated*. This is certainly one piece of information to look for while interviewing your relatives. Remember that church membership didn't always stay constant through the generations. Also, it wasn't historically uncommon to have but one church per town.

o *determining where the records kept by that church are today*. If the original church still exists, write them. Even if they don't still have their early records, they may be able to refer you to the present-day record-guardian. Local historical societies, libraries, or archives may have them. Use the *church records(and registers)* subject heading in your library research to locate published and microfilmed church records. The earlier-mentioned "Church Records" chapter in *The Source* is good; also E. Kay Kirkham's *Survey of American Church Records: Major and Minor Denominations, before 1880–1890* (Everton, 4th ed., 1978). Some church address sources are in Chapter 15.

Those researching their pre-American ancestors often enjoy better success with Church records. Because most other countries had national churches until a century or two ago, those records were not only well-kept, but usually covered a large segment of the population. For some countries and time-periods almost everybody will be included in the records of one national church, while in other countries and time-periods, there will be one or several non-conformist churches with large memberships to also consider.

Ireland, as one example of the latter situation, had besides her three largest churches (Roman Catholic, the *Established*, or Anglican, Church, and Presbyterian) several other large dissenting groups such as Baptists, Methodists, Huguenots, Methodists, and Quakers. Due to political, legal, and historical factors, it was often expedient to change or conceal one's church membership. Because of extreme harassment, Roman Catholics were particularly liable to. So if your ancestors aren't found on the church registers of what was thought to be the family's religion, they may yet be found on the state religion, Church of Ireland registers (also known as the *Established*, or Anglican, Church). And, of course, possibilites for church membership vary from northern to southern Ireland. As this example implies, it's certainly helpful, if not necessary, to learn not only the religious background of your ancestors, but something of the religious history of the country or area you will be researching as well.

CEMETERY RECORDS

Cemetery records are another good source of vital statistics and include: *tombstone inscriptions, sexton,* or *custodian, records,* and *mortuary* (including *mortician* and *mausoleum) records.* The latter are usually the best, so use them whenever available (they go back to post-civil war times). Check the *National Directory of Morticians* (Youngstown, OH: National Directory of Morticians, annual), available at large libraries or through a local mortuary, for names and addresses of the mortuaries and funeral homes in this country. Many early records are published, and later records, often quite complete, can be obtained from the appropriate funeral home by request of a close relative.

For earlier time periods, sexton records for the town, city, county, and sometimes for private or national cemeteries, should be considered first. They are generally more complete, and less prone to error than the headstones. If your ancestor was buried in a church cemetery, as so many were in earlier times, than those burial records are often found with other church records.

Head- or tombstones are worth checking, although many, disappointingly, give initials, rather than names of the deceased, or have mistakes. Presently there are volumes of books or transcripts containing tombstone records; use these when available. Transcripts put out by the Scottish Genealogical Society for the monumental tombstone inscriptions of their pre-1855 cemeteries (this being the date when Scottish vital registration began) are examples of some that are well-done. Besides being indexed and arranged by gravestone location; also included are pertinent county and cemetery maps, and a description of emblems, drawings, and other tombstone markings. Many books are less well-done, and often are only alphabetical listings.

In any case, nothing compares to an actual visit to see the headstone and its surrounding graves. Many times relationships will emerge from a careful notice of the family burials. The Jones buried in one end of the cemetary are obviously of a different family than the contemporary Jones found in the other end. And a Brown found buried amongst a large group of Smiths certainly had some family ties with them.

Tombstones may also turn out to be the only source for learning certain important facts, such as a maiden names; the original form of a surname later americanized; or data about children dying young (a good-sized percentage of the pre-twentieth century population). In areas of great civil strife, such as parts of Ireland and the southern states, tombstone records may take on added value as the only remaining record of the dead.

> **Visiting an ancestral cemetery may be one of the most interesting and (sometimes) productive experiences you'll have.**

For a variety of reasons, then, search the local cemeteries in each known ancestral residence whenever possible. Examine the death certificates or obituary notices of each family member to learn which cemeteries were used by the family. Then look up those locations in a county history or on older county or city maps. Chambers of Commerce, City halls, older citizens, the known owner of the cemetery itself, but *especially* the local funeral homes can also help you locate a particular cemetery.

Background research into burial laws and customs will yield facts of interest. Quakers, e.g., didn't use tombstones, and in some Southern states burials were above-ground because of the high water table. Also, because tombstone design styles have varied, these can help you approximate the time of erection (thus enabling you to judge better whether the deathdate recorded on the tombstone can be considered as primary, or secondary evidence of that fact). As family burial patterns varied among the different ethnic groups, these can also suggest country of origin if that is unknown (see *The Source* for details).

To visit an ancestral cemetery, wear working clothes and old shoes or boots, avoid early morning or dusk if snakes may be a problem, and bring the following: pen, paper; chalk, flour, soapstone, or pellon (a nonwoven fabric) for making rubbings; a camera; stiff-bristled, non-wire brush for cleaning; tweezers to remove lichen or other debris on the inscription, and clippers for removing branches and weeds. And be careful in handling very old gravestones. In the eastern USA, the climate has worn away many of the most ancient. Some have been restored, but there is then an even greater likelihood of transcribing errors. In Europe, you may find graveyards several centuries old and still in fine condition.

OTHER SOURCES FOR VITAL STATISTICS

Vital records, of course, are not infallible. Mistakes occur in every type of record, at least occasionally. Generally, however, they occur less in direct, primary sources, of which vital records are a prime example, than anywhere else; that is why you'll want to begin your original research by examining them. But don't forget that other record categories sometimes yield at least secondary evidence regarding vital statistics. Here are examples:

o   The official Anglican church of pre-Revolutionary Virginia performed several civil functions, such as assigning out the duty to walk over the private property boundaries within the parish, known as *processioning*. A dated processioning record entry noting that John Smith replaces William Campbell as a processioner because of the latter's death, provides you with primary, direct evidence for this William's deathdate. By going back to the earlier entry that appointed William to this assignment, the time of his death may be narrowed to a period of a few weeks or less. (To record a death date for a person known to be alive at one time and dead at another: "between 1 June 1800 and 27 July 1801." If the two dates refer to when the will was written, and when it was recorded or proved, then write as: "w.d.(will dated) 1 June 1800, w.p.(will proved) 27 July 1801."

o   A dated court order book entry may read: "Thomas Nixon petitioned court for inheritance due his bride, Mary Stucky, from estate of her uncle Edmund Allen, dec'd." Here is evidence of a marriage year; also, evidently, of the wife's maiden name (sometimes, though, this may be a middle name. Other research may be needed to determine which is the case). And looking through earlier probate records for her uncle's will may well yield additional facts about her family.

This revelation of excellent genealogical facts and clues in miscellaneous and unexpected sources is not uncommon. That is why, when vital records aren't available for one of your ancestors, you'll probably want to eventually search *every* record category you can locate, in case some valuable information may be found therein. But, of course, you will work with the law of averages by first checking out these more obvious sources.

> **Finding unexpected, helpful facts in miscellaneous sources is a fairly common, but always exciting, occurance.**

SUMMARY

You'll want to look carefully for the vital statistics generally found in family, government, church, or cemetery records. Even when unavailable, however, other searches may well yield desired data; the next two chapters will examine some of these helpful sources.

Chapter 12. COURT, LAND, AND CENSUS RECORDS

COURT RECORDS

Wills & Probates are generally the first court records to check. They often give circumstantial, if not direct, evidence of relationships. Unmarried, or childless, people may name nieces and nephews as heirs (an example of how you may benefit by researching the siblings of each ancestor). And we also often gain valuable evidence connecting maternal lines if the deceased person names married daughters or their children.

However, not all children (in some cases, not any) may be named in a will; children dying before their parent, or having already received their inheritance are especially likely to be left out. See if you can supplement children's names by looking for possible *deeds of gift* made before, or *quit claim deeds* made after, the parent's death. (The latter are usually complete in naming all then-living children.) Also note when grandchildren are named heirs in will or land records. Often they are receiving the portion of inheritance due a deceased parent.

The eldest son may not be named in some early wills, as the English law of *primogeniture* (providing him automatic inheritance, unless otherwise specified in the father's will) was followed by these colonies until the Revolutionary War: New York, New Jersey, Virginia, North and South Carolina and Georgia. (Rhode Island abolished primogeniture in 1770; Maryland replaced it with *equal division* (each child receiving equally when the father's will didn't otherwise specify) in 1715; and Pennsylvania, Delaware and the New England colonies all granted equal divisions, with the eldest son, if any, to be given a double share.)

The farther back you research in this country, the more valuable will records become. Land and probate generally were the only records regarded as crucial when the main concerns were conquering a wilderness and survival. Also, because most early Americans were landholders, they were more motivated to leave a will. Even when they didn't, other required probate records can help. Learning the *executor(s)* or *administrator(s)* (Appendix E for definitions; they were invariably close relatives) may obviously help you identify an unknown family of origin. Or an entire surviving family can be reconstituted through *lists of surviving relatives* sometimes more recently required.

Start by searching for ancestral wills; then for supplementary court records.

Most often the wills and probate records are found in the county where the person died. (Remember, as is still true, widows and widowers often lived with, or visited among, their children, and so may not have died where they earlier lived.) Everton's *Handy Book* again gives desired specifics: which USA counties have their probate records, for which years, and title of the record-keeper in charge. Will and probate records are usually alphabetized and indexed by the deceased person's surname, so aren't difficult to locate whether by personal courthouse visit; or by examining the microfilmed index, and then requesting the desired photocopies from the county clerk. A few indexes are still unmicrofilmed. If you can't personally examine them; request by correspondence. Include a check for $3-4, ask for complete entries for the surname in all indexes, and the cost for photocopies. Then cross your fingers. If the indexed entries are sent, examine these to see which would be worth photocopying. (The GSU has microfilmed most indexes, but seldom the probate packets themselves. These are helpful; often being worth a personal courthouse visit if necessary.)

Sometimes the county will have its will records abstracted, well-indexed, and published. This not only simplifies, but greatly expands your search possibilities, allowing you to find other wills where your relatives are mentioned. Many a maternal surname as thus been uncovered. We'll say, for example, that your ancestors Edward and Sarah McMullen were known to reside in Botetourt Co., Virginia in 1780. You learn this was a break-off of Augusta Co., and during your library research you find Augusta Co.'s pre-1800 abstracted, indexed and published court records. In looking up *McMullen* in the index, among other items, you find a Sarah McMullen named as daughter of James Robinson in his will dated 1770. (Of course, you may also then need to rule out any other contemporary Sarah McMullens before you could qualify yours alone as this Sarah Robinson McMullen.)

Other Court Records: Besides probate, courts have a large variety of other legal records, such as naturalization (see next chapter), divorce, trespass, debt, etc. Any time you learn of an Anglo ancestor involved in a lawsuit, or if a situation likely to have resulted in litigation is noted (such as a family feud or contested will), do whatever is necessary to gain access to the resulting court records, because England traditionally relied heavily upon its judicial system, even to resolving family quarrels. Colonial America followed suit, thus producing voluminous, and often genealogically-relevant, court record proceedings. Colonial and early state court *order books* (often microfilmed) are especially helpful and will often even be worth the sometimes-necessary page-by-page searching.

Many early state *court of appeals* record abstracts are published, and early court order books and other records are either published (as transcripts or abstracts) or microfilmed. If the microfilming was done by the GSU, you'll find them through the GSU *Locality Catalog*, if by the court itself, locate them in the state archives, and/or the county office. Most modern court records, though, are still in the original jurisdiction, and each state has a separate and distinct court system. Greenwood's *The Researcher's Guide to American Genealogy* and *The Source* provide information to search these, should you need to.

LAND RECORDS

Value: Because most colonists acquired property, because genealogical facts are often included, and because of their excellent legal value, land sale records make up an extremely useful source for early USA researchers. It's not unusual to find a chain of title in 18th century and earlier deeds that take a pedigree back for some generations. Researchers of this early period may even find it more productive to trace the descent of land known to belong to their family, than to trace the descent of their ancestors directly. For researching abroad, land records may still be valuable. While there were fewer landowners, yet often the names of those working the land are included.

Jurisdictions: Federal, state, or county jurisdictions at different times have been involved in land sales, and in colonial times each colony handled land transactions differently. We will provide here a basic, brief, overview:

1. **State Land Records**: Land records for the 13 original colonies are now on the state or local level. Many compilations and indexes (some excellent) have been done; be on the look-out for these doing your library research. Our early Virginia research was greatly helped, for instance, by the use of Nugent's *Cavaliers and Pioneers: Abstracts of Virginia Land Patents and Grants, 1623-1732*, a 3 volume indexed work of over 80,000 genealogically pertinent entries.

Because *Maine* was part of Massachusetts until 1820, *Vermont* was part of New York until 1791, *Kentucky* (in 1792) and *West Virginia* (in 1863) were both created from Virginia, and *Tennessee*, from North Carolina in 1792; therefore, look for their pre-statehood land records in their parent (rather than their own) state archives. *Texas* (a Republic, with its own land records before statehood) has in its Austin General Land Office, indexed records back to 1745 from the Spanish Archives. For all these states, then and the *13 Original Colonies*, land records are in the individual (or parent) state. The National DAR Library has the best collection of these (sometimes indexed) land records.

2. **Federal Land Records**: At the close of the Revolutionary War, several states claiming land west of the Mississippi River, ceded it over to the new national government as *public domain* land. Other western land was later ceded to, or purchased by, the United States. The following *public land* states were formed from this area: Alabama, Alaska, Arkansas, Arizona, California, Colorado, Florida, Idaho, Illinois, Indianna, Iowa, Kansas, Louisiana, Michigan, Minnesota, Misssippi, Missouri, Montana, Nebraska, Nevada, New Mexico, North Dakota, Ohio, Oklahoma, Oregon, South Dakota, Utah, Washington, Wisconsin, and Wyoming. The land records in the National Archives consist principally of documents relating to initial land sale or disposal in these states. So if your ancestor was a first settler of a piece of land in any of the above states (unless buying from a state government, speculator, or railroad, which occasionally happened) you can probably find record of his original land purchase in the National Archives. Consult one of the following sources (also good for census, military, migration, and naturalization records):

o Babbel, June A., *Lest We Forget, a Guide to Genealogical Research in The Nation's Capital)* 5th ed., rev. Annandale, VA: The Author, 1982. (Essential reference for researching in our Capitol. Covers holdings of, and how to research in the National Archives, Library of Congress, DAR and NGS Libraries.)

o *Guide to Genealogical Research in the National Archives*, National Archives Trust Fund Board: Wash. DC, 2nd ed., 1983.

o *Genealogical Records in the United States*, Research Paper Series B, No.1., 1978 (from GSU). Good; considers 31 types of records for USA research, including land.

The federal land records date mainly from 1800 to 1973. But there is very little genealogical information on their *land entry papers* until the *Homestead Act* was passed in 1862. Some other early federal land records do have good information, however, including the *donation entry files* for Florida, (1842-1850) Oregon, and Washington (1851-1903, with microfilmed indexes) and *private land claims* for parts of Alabama, Arizona, Arkansas, California, Colorado, Florida, Illinois, Indiana, Iowa, Louisiana, Michigan, Missipi, Missouri, New Mexico, and Wisconsin. The latter record group is of individuals claiming grants from the pre-USA governments holding the Northwest and Mississippi Territories; the Louisiana Purchase; and the Florida and Mexican Cessions.

3. **County Land Records**: After the federally-owned (public domain) land was first sold, the state was then responsible for subsequent sale and tax records. These later deeds are often indexed and on the county level, again making them readily accessible whether searching in the courthouse, in the microfilmed indexes (found through the *Locality Catalog*) or corresponding with a county clerk. Everton's *Handy Book* again gives dates of extant county deeds, and addresses and titles to write for them. Generally there are two sets of indexes: grantor (seller) and grantee (buyer). The first grantee deed may indicate, if not identify, the prior residence of a newcomer. Likewise, the last grantor deed may indicate to whence he was moving, if sold in preparation for leaving. And sometimes the whole history of the land's descent (establishing genealogical descent also) is given. Look for these additional possibilities: names of relatives (participating parties often are); wife's given (and, only occasionally, maiden) name; deathdates; perhaps circumstantial evidence by which approximate dates of birth and marriage can be figured; and occupation or social status.

In many cases, the earliest known county of residence is the logical place to begin a land record search. Evidence found there may then lead you to earlier county, federal or state sources. If you can't find the original grantee deed for your ancestor's land, then it was likely inherited. Look for evidence of this in his father's (or another relative's) will, or in a property division recorded under his surname. If not found through these sources, then the land probably descended through his wife's family, and you'll want to search for that proof.

Look for and ask about *platte books* for the county. These contain the old land surveys and related facts. Also often found with county land records are *power of attorney* papers that furnish evidence of relationships, and maybe family migration patterns. A power of attorney given by George Brown of Logan Co., West Virginia to Cyrus Brown to sell land for him in Hard Rock, Kansas, gives circumstantial evidence of a relationship, as well as another county to research (in this case, Logan may turn out to be a prior residence of your Browns.)

A final tip may help if an ancestor's prior home cannot otherwise be determined:

> **If all else fails, trace back the associates of your ancestor to their place of origin, and you may find your ancestor there with them.**

This often works because the common pattern was for extended families, or even whole neighborhoods (most common for families of germanic descent) to migrate together.

CENSUS RECORDS

Early 1790-1840: Although these early American census records don't give the names and birthplaces of those enumerated, they do disclose the name of the "head of the family" as well as the number, sex, and approximate ages of those living with him. This age grouping data often helps you to approximate ages of at least some family members as you trace them through successive censuses. Even more importantly, these early censuses provide help because they are now all indexed. Printed and microfiched census indexes can thus can be used as finding tools when you know only the name of your ancestor.

Realize, however, several states are missing some, or at least some parts of, their federal censuses. For the states Virginia, Kentucky, Georgia, Tennessee, New Jersey, and Delaware, for example, various other records (mostly state tax) of a corresponding time period have been indexed and substituted for their missing 1790 census. (Tax records, by the way, supplement censuses by including unmarried property-owners, or those living with another family; while censuses include non-propertied families. So search both, if available.)

1850-1870: Beginning with the 1850 census, names, ages, and birthplaces of all those enumerated (as well as occupation of males over 15, value of real estate, and some other helpful items) are included. Thus, the federal censuses from that year on allow us to reconstitute family groups, often completely. Especially now that each state's 1850 census has been indexed, this has greatly increased their research value. The 1860 adds to these facts the value of personal property, while the 1870 importantly indicates "foreign" for parents born abroad. Some states have these censuses in book form (such as the Tennessee 1850 and 1860 censuses, and the West Virginia 1880 census). Also, you may want to be put on the mailing lists of the following active indexing firms:

Index Publishing, POB 11467, Salt Lake City, UT 84147, who claim some one-third more names than appear on comparable indexes, by early 1987 had *COM copies for sale of the following censuses: 1848-50 Ontario, Canada; 1860 federal censuses for California, Connecticut, Delaware, Washington, DC, Florida, Kentucky, Oregon, Rhode Island, South

Carolina (every-name); and 1870 federal censuses for Delaware, Washington, DC, Florida (every-name), Oregon and Rhode Island. Their prices range from $10 to $216, depending on the size of the state and numbers involved.

Accelerated Index Searching, International (AIS), 225 N. Hwy 89, Suite 1, No. Salt Lake City, UT 84054, has published even many more censuses than the above. They claim to be presently expanding their 50 million name online database by some 600,00 entries per month. In 1987 they are beginning a *Computer Interface Club* to make available for online searching the same part of that database already available as COM copies in the branch genealogical system of the GSU (see Chapter 2. The service is somewhat expensive; write them for details.)

1880: The 1880 census can provide excellent help. For one thing, it finally provides direct evidence of each person's exact relationship to the head of the household. (Keep in mind, however, the wife of the head of the household, as she may not be his first wife, is therefore not necessarily mother of all, or any, of his children.) Those enumerated also stated the state or country of their own and their parents' birth. If reported accurately, this will help you trace back further generations. But, as secondary evidence, it may not be completely trustworthy. (For example, in a Tennesse family we researched, the son reported his mother's birthplace as Alabama while she, living as a widow within his household, then reported her birthstate as Tennessee, while on an earlier census she reported it as Virginia!)

Besides these advantages, the 1880 census has a partial "soundex" index (this means all names sounding alike are together; it is not difficult to use, if included instructions are closely followed). This soundex covers all families with children aged 10 or under. Microfilmed copies are available through the GSU, the National Archives, and their respective branches. As mentioned in Chapter 2, the GSU is also now computerizing the 1880 census to be one of the resource files making up the GIS. It will be the equivalent of an online every-name, every-state index and will provide us with the easiest way yet to access and use this census.

Special schedules 1850-1880: An agricultural census and special mortality schedules accompanied the 1850-1880 censuses. The latter, especially, as it provides detailed data of those dying within the year previous, is of genealogical value. Many mortality schedules have been recently published, constituting one of the *AIS Indexes*.

1890 and Later: The 1890 census, unfortunately, was destroyed, except for parts of 17, mostly western, counties (about 1% of the total census), and except for a schedule of Civil War Union veterans or their widows living in states alphabetically from Kentucky (part) to Wyoming. Those veteran schedules are available as *COM from *Index Publishing*.

The 1900 and 1910 censuses are both recently available on microfilm at the National Archives or through its branches. The 1900 census supplies for the only time *birth month and year* for all enumerated. It is also completely indexed (as will be the 1920 census when released; scheduled for 1992). The 1910 census, as the most recently available, will certainly be valuable to many now "stuck" in the early twentieth century, or whose ancestors immigrated between 1900 and 1910. It also supplies number of years married, number of previous marriages, and if a veteran. Both censuses give total number of children borne by the wife, how many of them are then living, and, where applicable, year of immigration.

The 1910 census, however, is indexed for 21 states only: Alabama, Arkansas, California, Florida, Georgia, Illinois, Kansas, Kentucky, Louisiana, Michigan, Missouri, Mississippi, North Carolina, Ohio, Oklahoma, Pennsylvania, South Carolina, Tennessee, Texas, Virginia, and West Virginia. (Additionally, *Index Publishing* has *COM copies for Nevada and West Virginia.) *Rights of privacy* laws prohibit releasing recent census data, which is regarded as confidential. Those who personally appear on the census, however, may request their data using a *Application for Search of Census Records*, from: U.S. Dept. of Commerce, Bureau of the Census, Personal Census Service Branch; Pittsburg, Kansas 66762

> **Because much indexing of the federal 1850–1920 censuses has been, or is being, done, researching that time period is becoming much easier.**

State, Colonial Censuses: States, colonies, counties, and cities sometimes conducted their own censuses, constituting a valuable, yet oft-neglected, resource. New York, as just one example, has some colonial and many state censuses for various of their counties published as books or microfilm. Those for 1892 and 1925 have card-indexes in the New York State Archives. Check for such resources when conducting your background research.

Census Locations: Part of the value of the federal censuses and their indexes lies in their easy accessibility. Many local city and county libraries have purchased at least their own state censuses, and often those for adjoining states as well. Your local librarian can help you find out if any nearby library has a desired census. You can also rent censuses from the GSU branch genealogical libraries, and rent or buy them through various libraries participating in the National Archives microfilmed census program. (Your librarian should have those details.) In some cases buying will be more economical; you may need to re-search it whenever a related surname is discovered, for instance.

Census-Searching Tips: To quickly locate a census entry, use *all* available indexes (as a check for errors; they are found in many large libraries). Record all data verbatim for every name in the ancestral household, as well as for possibly related neighbors. If an initial search for a family on a census is unsuccessful; a second, more-careful, search may be needed in which each entry is re-checked to make sure it is *not* the desired one. Doing this on a Canadian census, for instance, enabled us to finally find the Cosgriff family we wanted; appearing under the surname *Coskery*, it had been originally overlooked.

Check each census in which a family may be expected to appear, and you will likely find additional facts, as well as better be able to estimate probable ages (those of adults are often inaccurate). Search-sheets, available at genealogical supply centers, are based on the columnar set-up of each census for more rapid and accurate recording. Read tips on deciphering handwriting found in Chapter 14. Sometimes excessive fading or damage may make it difficult, if not impossible, to read. Fortunately, a new technology, *image enhancement*, can actually restore readability; and may soon be so used, according to recent reports by the National Archives.

Other Countries: 1841 is the first census for England, Wales and Scotland to give each persons' name, age, occupation, and country birthplace. The 1851 and every subsequent census adds relationship to household head, marital status, and exact English county or foreign country birthplace. The 1841-1881 censuses are microfilmed and available through the GSU and its branch genealogical libraries. The 1851 censuses are being indexed and many transcripts for the large English cities are already available. Many other countries likewise have microfilmed censuses and can be located through the Locality Catalog. Some microfilmed censuses for Spanish-speaking countries, for instance, began earlier, and contain more complete information, than those of English-speaking countries.

SUMMARY

There is a wealth of genealogical value in court, land, and census records. Use them!

Chapter 13. MILITARY, NATURALIZATION, AND IMMIGRATION RECORDS

MILITARY RECORDS

Two kinds of military records exist: service and pension. The latter often give good genealogical data; check them first.

> **Fortunately for USA researchers, millions of pension files (most with alphabetical name indexes) are found in the National Archives**

Pre-1850, including Revolutionary War, records: The few surviving military records predating the Revolutionary War have generally been published. *The Index of Revolutionary War Pension Applications* (NGS, 1966), a widely-found reference, indexes all the pension applications and related papers in the National Archives. Examine these microfilmed copies in person at the National Archives or order photocopies by mail using NATF Form 80 (obtain from the Reference Services Branch (NNIR), General Services Administration, Washington, DC 20408) and a $5.00 minimum charge. Supply required identification for them to locate the file, and request *all* documents in file; otherwise they provide selected copies, and may leave out something pertinent. Additionally, many states are having their pension applications published.

The Daughters of the American Revolution (DAR) have done the greatest work for non-pensioned veterans. Their *Lineage Books*, and 2 volume *Patriot Index*, (Washington, DC: DAR, 1966, 1979) are also widely available. Because this War included men older than all other (with the possible exception of Confederate soldiers in the Civil War, also a war of survival) many didn't survive to collect pensions. Microfilmed copies of pensioners in the War of 1812 (lasting until 1815) and the Mexican War (1846-1848) are available through the GSU, the National Archives, and their respective branches.

Post-1850 records, including Civil War: There are pensioners indexes for the Indian Wars (1892-1926) and Old Wars (1815-1925) in the National Archives. The Civil War again involved a large proportion of the country's manpower. It generated numerous records about its (Union) military personnel, and even about some civilians; (see Chapter 10 in the previously-mentioned *Guide to Genealogical Research in the National Archives*, hereafter referred to as "the National Archives *Guide*"--for records relating to civilians, mostly Confederates) at the same time it caused destruction of many earlier state and county records.

The General Index to Pensioners, 1861-1934 is a good source when pensions resulted. Confederate soldiers weren't generally included, but some Confederate service records have been published in the form of master's or doctoral theses. (Locate these latter through *Knowledge Index*, see p.47). And the names and regiments of Virginia Conferedate soldiers and sailors taken from a number of sources are currently being edited by Forrest Tucker. They are expected to comprise some 22 volumes, the first (covering surnames beginning with "A") to appear in 1987.

World War I draft registration cards for the entire country are located in the Atlanta, GA Archives Branch (address found in Appendix D) as Record Group 163 of Records of the Selective Service System (World War I). These are genealogically valuable, and cover probably 99% of the draft-age men. This is therefore an excellent USA source for many working from that time period backward. As they are arranged alphabetically by local board, you'll need to know an approximate residence within the state to use them effectively. If your ancestor served professionally in this country's military, consult the National Archives *Guide* to find valuable data in their microfilms, and use the subject heading *Military History* to find published records.

Other Countries: There are good military records abroad. And because a larger percentage of the population may have served in the military, these sources often turn out to be even more valuable than those for this country. Military censuses used to identify eligible servicemen exist for the Russian and Austrian Empire, as well as for Britain, Germany, and France. Muster rolls generally began from the mid-17th century. These not only give helpful genealogical data, but are often unique in providing such descriptive data as the soldier's complexion, height, and eye color.

NATURALIZATION RECORDS

The process of receiving citizenship is known as naturalization; where records of that process were kept, they are often an excellent source for the family involved. Until December, 1972, there were restrictions on USA naturalization information. But now you may obtain uncertified naturalization record copies from clerks of court. For the majority of United States immigrants, naturalization proceedings are court records.

> **Finding naturalization records granted before Sept. 27, 1906, is often a problem.**

On that date the Bureau of Immigration and Naturalization was established, and procedures became standardized. Here are possible locations of naturalization records for the following time periods:

1. Colonial times: A few naturalization records of this time (mostly oaths of allegiance) have been found and published. These, however, cover only a very small percentage of the population as the British maintained very few such records. Sometimes, however, you can find the place of origin of your colonial immigrant ancestor mentioned in such records as county court; wills; family Bibles, letters, histories, or traditions; voting rolls; land/ property; newspaper; and military.

2. Revolutionary War period to 1906: Not much exists before 1802 when aliens were required to register upon arrival (that act repealed in 1828, however). Even though more complete from that time, records are difficult to locate because either state, federal, or local courts might have been used. Although some indexes exist, you usually need to know when and where citizenship was granted before finding those documents.

If you know the county where the declaration of intention was made, or where the final papers were issued, that county courthouse will be the most likely location of those documents; begin your search there. Do so by visiting the courthouse personally, whenever possible. Naturalization records tend to be to be the most poorly organized court records; thus, persistent legwork by you and a cooperative clerk may be necessary to track them down. It's usually unsuccessful, then, to simply request them by a letter to the clerk of the court.

If the proceedings took place in a federal court, the resulting documents usually ended up in the National Archives. The branch nearest your ancestral residence is the next logical place to look for them. The 3rd chapter of the National Archives *Guide* will help; it provides specifics on various of these records under state-by-state listings, both for this and later time periods. There are also naturalization collections for various northeastern states:

o   Stevenson, J.R. "Persons Naturalized in New Jersey, 1702-1766," in *New York Genealogical & Biographical Record*, vol. 28, 1897.

o   *New Jersey Naturalization Records from 1740-1810*. Available in the New Jersey State Library Archives and History Division, 185 W. State St., Trenton, NJ 08625.

o   *Connecticut, Maine, Massachusetts, New Hampshire, Rhode Island Naturalizations Records from 1790-1906* (with a soundex card index) are in the National Archives.

o   *New York City Naturalization Records from 1792-1906*. Available, together with an index, in the New York archives branch.

o   *Massachusetts Naturalization Records from 1885-1931*. Available in the Archives Division at the State House in Boston, MS 02133.

o   Wyand, Jeffrey A., and Florence L. *Colonial Maryland Naturalizations* Baltimore: Genealogical Publishing Co. 1975.

3. Naturalization records after 1906: From Sept. 27, 1906, the records are much easier to locate, and contain valuable information. The first document made was known as a *Declaration of Intention*. If not filed at the port of entry; it was usually filed at the time of, or shortly following, the immigrant's arrival. *Final Papers* were made some 3-5 years later, so the two sets of documents are often filed in different places. Below is the required data for these documents, but how specifically the facts were given depended, of course, on the conscientious of the clerk involved:

o   *Declaration of Intention* (or *First Papers*, may have been filed even if citizenship process not completed): name; age; occupation; personal desciption; place/date of birth; citizenship; present and last foreign address; vessel/port of embarkation for USA; port/date of arrival in USA; application date; and signature.

o   *Final Papers* which include:

1. *Petition*: name; residence; occupation; date/place of birth; citizenship, personal desciption; emigration date; ports of embarkation/ arrival; marital status; names/ages/birthplaces of spouse and children; date/ port/name of ship of entry; names of witnesses; time of residence in state; name changes; and (after 1930) often a photograph.

2. *Certificates of Naturalization* and 3. *Oaths of Allegiance*: name, address, birthplace or nationality; country of emigration; birthdate or age; age; personal description; marital status; name/age or birthdate/address of spouse; names/ages/addresses of children.

Copies of these post-1906 naturalization proceedings (originally filed in any of several courts) are maintained in this office:

Immigration and Naturalization Service
425 Eye St. NW
Washington, DC 20536

Direct inquiries to them, using form G-641 (available from any *Immigration and Naturalization Service office*, given in your local phonebook under "USA Federal Government") and a $5.00 non-refundable fee for each name requested.

Several federal censuses (1820-30-70, 1900-10) and some state censuses provide citizenship status data. A voting list with your ancestor's name, not only provides proof of citizenship, but sometimes give date and place citizenship was granted, helping you to track down those documents.   Other records that sometimes give clues as to citizenship status are: tax lists, newspaper obituaries, deeds, and family papers.

Not all immigrants obtained citizenship, and many who did may have delayed past the minimum time (usually 5 years) required. Also, certain groups weren't allowed citizenship in our early history (Chinese being excluded for the longest time).   Until 1922, the wife and minor children automatically became citizens when the husband/father was naturalized.

IMMIGRATION

All Americans, even including our natives, have originated elsewhere. It used to be that the farther back in time you researched, the more difficult it was to find those origins. Fortunately, however, there has been much recent progress in compiling and indexing myriad scattered passenger and immigration lists. (The publication dates in our Bibliography prove how much of the work was done within the past decade.) For now, the largest published index (the *Passenger and Immigration Lists Index*, with 1,500,000 names published through 1986, and another million waiting to be) is most complete for pre-1825 years.

Those wishing to trace immmigrant ancestors arriving since then will be pleased to know of an important computerized immigration project now being compiled under the direction of Dr. Ira Glazier, Director of the Center of Immigration Research at Temple University. Data is being derived from the original passenger lists held by the National Archives for some 35 million immigrants who came to America by ship in the 1820-1924 time-period (with descendants estimated to number some 100 million).   No target date has been given for completion of this project, nor is its unpublished data open to the public.   Nevertheless, excellent publications have already resulted.

For example, 7 volumes entitled *Famine Immigrants* cover previously unindexed lists of Irish immigrants arriving in New York from 1846-51 (including 560,000 names) and were recently published from this database. Data for Germans arriving 1850-55 are the next scheduled volumes (the first of several segments expected to cover our largest immigrant group of the 19th century; some 700,000 Germans came during just those six years!) Some of these volumes are due to be published in 1987. Another work to include data on late 19th century East European immigrants has begun. Smaller-scale computerized immigration projects are also being done for specific ethnic groups, such as the Pennsylvania German, English Quakers, and the Swedish.

A mistake beginners often make is in trying to research the country of origin of the immigrant family too soon. Because it is necessary to know specific residence in the *old country* to successfully research there; and because knowing the names of relatives and associates will also help; a thorough search for these, and other identifying facts, should be made in all available American records *first*. Of course, the IGI is one international source that can be routinely examined early in your search. It often helps in figuring out a general, if not specific, residence. And *The Source* also has very detailed, helpful information (including a country-by-country summary of tools and bibliographies) in it's chapter, *Tracking Immigrant Origins*.

Many records pertaining to the country of your immigrant ancestor's birth may be as (sometimes more) accessible to you here, as abroad. More than one unfortunate has spent considerable time and money to locate and then research in overseas records, only to later discover these same records had already been microfilmed by the GSU.

Here is a current bibliography of passenger and immigration lists. While not complete, it demonstrates the great number of recent compilations of immigration material, including early passenger lists, we now have. The figures in parentheses is the approximate number of immigrant names listed, if known.

IMMIGRATION LIST BIBLIOGRAPHY

Wareing, John. *Emigrants to America: Indentured Servants Recruited in London, 1718–1733.* Baltimore: Genealogical Publishing Co., 1985. (1,500)

Tepper, Michael. *Emigrants to Pennsylvania, 1641–1819: a Consolidation of Ship Passenger Lists from the "Pennsylvania Magazine of History and Biography" (1877–1934).* Baltimore: Gen. Pub. Co., 1975. (7,000)

_____. *Passengers to America: a Consolidation of Ship Passenger Lists from the "New England Historical and Genealogical Register" (1847–1961)* Baltimore: Genealogical Publishing Co., 1977. (18,000)

_____. *Immigrants to the Middle Colonies: a Consolidation of Ship Passenger Lists and Associated Data from the "New York Genealogical and Biographical Record," (1879–1970).* Baltimore: Gen. Pub. Co., 1978 (6,000)

_____. *New World Immigrants: a Consolidation of Ship Passenger Lists and Associated Data from Periodical Literature.,* 2 vols. Baltimore: Gen. Pub. Co., 1980. (25,000)

_____. *Passenger Arrivals at the Port of Baltimore 1820–1834 from Customs Passenger Lists.* Baltimore: Gen. Pub. Co., 1982. (50,000)

_____. *Passenger Arrivals at the Port of Philadelphia, 1800–1819.* Baltimore: Gen. Pub. Co., 1985. (40,000)

Glazier, Ira and Tepper, Michael (eds). *The Famine Immigrants: Lists of Irish Immigrants Arriving at the Port of New York, 1846–1851.* 7 vol. Baltimore: Gen. Pub. Co., 1983–6. (560,000)

Glazier, Ira and Filby, P. William (eds). *Lists of German Immigrants Arriving at all Ports in America.* Wilmington: Scholarly Resources. Due 1987.

Directory of Scottish Settlers in North America, 1625–1825 by David Dobson. 6 vol. Baltimore: Genealogical Publishing Co. 1980–6. (25,000)

Boyer, Carl. III. *Ship Passenger Lists: National and New England (1600–1825).* 3rd pr. The Compiler, Newhall, CA. 1980. (9,000)

_____. *Ship Passenger Lists: New York and New Jersey (1600–1825)* 3rd pr. The Compiler, Newhall, CA. 1983. (10,000)

_____. *Ship Passenger Lists: The South (1538–1825).* 3rd pr. The Compiler, Newhall, Calif., 1983. (11,000)

_____. *Ship Passenger Lists: Pennsylvania and Delaware (1641–1825).* 3rd pr. The Compiler, Newhall, CA. 1984. (8,000)

English Origins of New England Families (extracted from *The New England Historical and Genealogical Register*). Two series; 6 vol. Baltimore: Genealogical Publishing Co. 1984–5.

Filby, P.Wm., with Meyer, Mary K. or Lower, Dorothy M. *Passenger and Immigration Lists*

Index and Annual Supplements. Gale Research Co., Detroit, 1981-7. (1,500,000) (very well-done, easy-to-use, widely-found source; consult it first for early immigrants).

Filby, P. Wm. *Passenger and Immigration Lists Bibliography 1538-1900* and *Supplement*. Published Lists of Arrivals in the USA and Canada. Gale Research Co., Detroit, 1981-4. (Supersedes Lancour's *Bibliography*, 1963)

_____. *Philadelphia Naturalization Records, an Index to Records of Aliens' Declarations of Intention and/or Oaths of Allegiance, 1789-1880*. Detroit: Gale Research Co. 1982. (120,000)

Coldham, Peter Wilson. *Bonded Passengers to America*. 9 vol. in 3. Baltimore: Genealogical Publishing Co. 1983. (52,000)

_____. *English Adventurers and Emigrants, 1609-1660. Abstracts of Examimations in the High Court of Admiralty with Reference to Colonial America*. Baltimore: Genealogical Publishing Co. 1984.

Swierenga. Robert P. *Dutch Emigrants to the U.S., South Africa, South America, and Southeast Asia, 1835-1880: an Alphabetrical Listing by Household Heads and Independent Persons*. Wilmington, Del., Scholarly Resources. 1983. (21,800)

_____. *Dutch Immigrants in U.S. Ship Passenger Manifests, 1820-1880: an Alphabetical Listing by Household Heads and Independent Persons*. 2 vols. Wilmington, Del.: Scholarly Resources, 1983. (55,000)

_____. *Dutch Households in US Population Censuses 1850-60-70: an Alphabetized Listing by Family Heads*. 2 vols. Wilmington, Del.: Scholarly Resources, 1987. (55,000)

Nimmo, Sylvia Lee. *Passenger Lists: Transcriptions from National Archives Copies Made by Michael Cassady*. Omaha, Nebraska. 1983. (15,000)

Newman, Harry Wright. *To Maryland from Overseas*. Baltimore: Genealogical Publishing Co. 1985. (1,400)

Holcomb, Brent H. *South Carolina Naturalizations, 1783-1850*. Baltimore: Genealogical Publishing Co. 1985. (7,500)

Strassberger, Ralph Beaver, and Hinke, William John. *Pennsylvania German Pioneers*. Baltimore: Genealogical Publishing Co. 1980.

Miller, Olga K. *Migration, Emigration, Immigration* Logan, UT: Everton Pub., 2 vols., 1974-81. (This last is a very good emigration sources bibliography.)

SUMMARY

Military, naturalization and immigration records can be quite valuable. In the past, and even now, these have been hard to locate. Yet much valuable gathering and indexing is being done. Most recently has this been true of the early American immigration records, helping to gradually dissolve the handicap with which USA researchers have long had to grapple. While success in crossing the ocean from this country to the homeland can never be guaranteed, yet by taking advantage of what is now available, your chances are certainly improving.

Chapter 14. INTERPRETING RECORDS: NAMES; SPELLING; LEGALITIES; ETC.

Written records must generally form the basis of our deductions. Yet, because all languages are subject to problems of ambiguity, it is sometimes hard to be sure of even a current author's intended meaning.

> We must take special care, then, in interpreting records made in a time or place unfamiliar to us.

NAMES

Names present us with both clues and problems. People whose names are spelled differently may yet be related, while those with an identical surname may not be. Take, for instance, our surname derived from the Gaelic word, *Coscraigh*. Because literacy was still uncommon in Ireland and spelling was not standardized before the late 19th century, and further depending on local dialect and preference of the recorder; the name could be written as *Cosgrove*, *Cosgrave*, *Cosgriff*, *Clusker*, *Cluskey*, *Cosgre(a)ve*, *Cosgrive*, *Cusko*, *Cusker(y)*, *Coskeran*, *Cosk(e)r(ry)*, *Crosgrave*, *McCosk(r)ery*, *McCusker*, *O'Coskery*, etc. These variants are unrelated to the English surname *Cosgrove*, of a completely different derivation.

Surname Origins: In general surnames came from: (1) rank or occupation, e.g.: *Cooper* or *Smith*; (2) location, e.g.: *Hill*, *Washington*, or *Holland* (the latter implying origins in that country, but living elsewhere when the surname taken); (3) description, e.g., *Armstrong* or *Read* (for red); (4) animal, vegetable, or mineral, e.g., *Fox* or *Silver*; (5) personal names, e.g., *Abraham* or *Dobkins* (affectionate form of *little Rob* in England), and including (6) patronymics:

patronymic	meaning		nationality
McDonald	descendent of Donald		Scottish
O'Conner	(or son of) Conner		Irish
Price	"	Rice	Welsh
(originally ap Rice)			
Evans	"	Evan	Welsh
Johnson	"	John	English
Rasmussen	"	Rasmus	Scandinavian
Andreiovich	"	Andrei	Russian

Fig. 7. Examples of Patronymics

Surnames & Work-History as Clues to Ethnic Origins: Many American names are variants of the immigrant's original European surname. There was social pressure, especially strong about the mid-19th century, to anglicize foreign-sounding names. Thus, in looking for a *Brown*, *Black*, *Carpenter*, *McInturf*, *Price*, *Peterson*, or *Noah*, keep your mind open to such possible original forms as *Braun*, *Schwartz*, *Zimmerman*, *Muckindorf*, *Preiss*, *Bieter* or *Noakowski*. We'll see later how to also allow for alternative spellings. A valuable appendix listing surname variations in the pre-20th century censuses is found in:

-US Bureau of the Census. *A Century of Population Growth, 1790-1900*. Repr. ed., NYC: Johnson Reprints, 1966.

Ethnic groups at various times in our history tended toward certain occupations; resulting in such stereotypes as the: Irish policeman, German mercenary, and Jewish scientist. Knowing your immigrant's work-history, along with the original surname form, may thus help uncover as yet undetermined ethnic background. Thomas Sowell's, *Immigrant America* (New York: Basic Books, 1981) gives background, including cultural, occupational, and personality patterns, for the largest American immigration groups: Irish, Scotch-Irish, German, Italian, Jewish, African and other Black, Japanese, Chinese, and Hispanic. Contrary to the popularly accepted, but inaccurate, *melting pot* myth, most groups married among themselves, usually for some generations following immigration.

As previously mentioned, a rare or localized surname in conjunction with a good finding aid (such as the AIS Indexes for the USA, and the IGI for many countries) in some cases will quickly lead you to place of origin. A student of ours with an uncommon surname, and little knowledge of his father's family, wanted to know from whence it had originated. By searching the AIS he immediately found that only North Carolina had many early listings).

Or, if all IGI entries for a maternal surname occur in only one German town, along with entries for the paternal surname, this might again provide good indication of the likely ancestral town. This is most convincing, of course, in countries where the IGI includes much of the early population, and where many surnames are localized (i.e., limited to a small area within the country, such as in Italy, and many germanic countries).

Christian Names and Naming Patterns as Clues: Saint names were adopted as first names throughout Europe as it was Christianized. However, naming practices developed differently. In some germanic countries a double baptismal name was given, and the first of these was often the same for all same-sexed children in a family. So a child went by his or her middle name. Also, given names varied in popularity from one country to another, according to who were the locally-popular kings, queens, or (often religious) heros and heroines (which is why Maria has been such a popular female name in Catholic countries).

Christian, or first, names provide important clues in early times, because families traditionally passed these down. A recent study comparing historical child-naming practices in a German and Massachusetts town found, for example, that naming the eldest son after the father, and the eldest daughter after the mother, was equally common in both cultures in the late 17th century, with the practice gradually declining in later generations.

Thus, it's possible to determine the likely country of origin simply by noting the names and naming practices used by a family around the time of immigration. Recurrence of the Christian name **Cornelius**, for example, hints towards either Dutch or Irish origins, being a popular name with both those ethnic groups. (If **Patrick** and **Michael** are also found, Irish descent is a strong possibility, while **Jan** and **Hendrick/Henry**) would indicate likely Dutch origins.) Or if all the children are double-named (before the mid-18th century when middle names became popular), they may well have been of Germanic origin.

First names were traditionally passed down from prior generations, and so can help us identify both country and family of origin.

A helpful naming pattern we found followed by the Scotch in about half the families we studied (and also common in other British countries) was to name the eldest son after the father's father; 2nd son after the mother's father; eldest daughter after the mother's mother;

2nd daughter after the father's mother. Often the pattern extended even further: 3rd son after father, 4th son after father's brother, 5th son after mother's brother, 3rd daughter after mother, 4th daughter after mother's sister, 5th daughter after father's sister.

Giving two living children in a family identical given names is quite rare; so finding a child same-named as an elder sibling, almost always indicates the elder of the two died before the second was named. A practice sometimes noted in large British and American families was using names derived from Roman numbers, sometimes indicating birth order: e.g., naming an eighth child *Octavious* (a boy) or *Octavia* (a girl). See what naming patterns you can uncover for your area of research.

USING NAMES AND OTHER EVIDENCE FOR IDENTIFICATION

Names by themselves are often inadequate at providing proof of descent. This fact will be readily appreciated if you attempt to conclusively trace the ancestry of a **William Smith** or **Mary Jones**. But less common names have also been misidentified. A **John Nott** born in Connecticut cannot be assumed identical, or even related, to a **John Nott** whose marriage record is found in Michigan some 50 years later, else serious errors may result. Avoid such naive assumptions by considering the name as circumstantial evidence only; then seek out other evidence to confirm or overrule that identity.

> **Names provide only circumstantial evidence of identity; search out other evidence to confirm that identity.**

Nicknames and Descriptive *Tags*: Because some names were so commonly shared, look for other identifying facts. Nicknames were common and help to establish identities in places with a limited supply of traditional Christian and surname combinations. A small Irish town, for instance, might have ten John Sullivans. Descriptive nickname were then used; e.g., *One-eyed John*, *Red John*, *Long John*, etc. Standard nicknames were even more commonly used; for example, *Eliza*, *Liz(zie)*, *Bess*, or *Betsy*, for **Elizabeth**; *Polly* or *Molly* for **Mary**; *Patsey* for **Martha**; *Peggy* for **Margaret**; *Sally* or *Sadie* for **Sarah**; *Fanny* for **Frances** or *Euphan* (a Scottish name) and *Nancy* or *Nannie* for **Ann**; *Anna* sometimes for **Hannah** or **Johannah**, and **Jean**, **Janet**, and **Joan** often interchangeable. Seek out these standard nicknames for the country where you are researching as they may not be obvious; **Owen** for **Eugene**, **Pierce** for **Peter**, and **Winifred** for **Unity**, e.g., are all equivalent Irish names.

Other means of identifications, such as occupation, age, family relationships, military rank, residence, personal description, ethnic group, or social class, were also commonly appended to the name. These *tags* help you distinguish between same-named neighbors. The following examples, drawn mainly from colonial America, are typical:

o Mary Smith, *daughter of William* (family).

o David Miller, *Tom's Creek* or *T.C.* (residence, often abbreviated;)

o *redhead* James Jones (description or nickname).

o John Paul, *carpenter* (occupation; note that an indexer might mistakenly include this tag as part of the name, and index this entry, e.g., as *John Paul Carpenter!*)

o *Capt*. Thomas Howard (military title; however, this particular title may also refer to ship captain, i.e., occupation).

o William Mosely, *dutchman* (ethnic group; often noted if relatively uncommon for that neighborhood. Because Germans were often called *Dutchmen*, a corruption of the German *Deutsch*, and if the name itself doesn't make it clear, you may need to study the local history to find if your *dutchman* ancestor was more likely Dutch or German.)

o Michael King, *Gent.* (abbreviation of *gentlemen* ; in early records, referred to families entitled to bear coat of arms. In later [especially colonial American] records, such titles are more nebulous, indicating only he was of the community's social elite.)

o Bruce Guernsey, *Jr.* (age; a later section will detail this designation).

o James Bradley, *dec'd* (abbreviation for *deceased*).

Be alert to note such designations. They not only help distinguish people of the same name; but, some provide clues leading to other records. A military title, for example, naturally suggests possible military records. *Gentlemen*, in early records, alerts you to possible coat-of-arms that may enable you to connect him to his overseas family of origin. And the use of *deceased* is evidence of a prior deathdate; search for earlier probate records.

Signatures, Marks, Slave Names, Coat-of-Arms: An authentic signature will ascertain whether a record pertains to your ancestor or not. But first examine adjacent records; if each has the same handwriting, then the signatures belonged to the county clerk, and so provide no identifying evidence. The many who were illiterate used a mark instead of a signature. (And even a literate person, if making a deathbed will, or if otherwise quite feeble, may also have used a mark.) The common *X* wouldn't help much. But people with common names often adopted more unique marks. And, if copied well enough by county clerks or record-abstractors, it could thus help you make positive identification.

Livestock brands (recorded in county records) provide similar means of identification, as does the previously mentioned coat-of-arms. The latter may not only provide the crucial link between the immigrant and his European family, but can also distinguish between families of the same surname within this, or another, country. Lastly, slave names, recorded in tax, deed, will, or other records, provide circumstantial evidence of descent and relationships among white slaveholders, as well as for black pedigrees. Many means of identification were thus used in addition to names. Be alert to, and make use of, these as needed.

Surnames Used as Christian Names: The use of saint names as Christian names continued unabated into modern times. But in England, and so also among the American colonists, a common practice for some centuries ago was to use the mother's maiden surname as name of a son (and, more rarely, of a daughter). Thus, parents John Smith and Mary Miles might name one of their sons Miles Smith. When Miles Smith married Ann, daughter of Edwin Dixon, they may name one son Dixon, another after the father, Miles, and others after grandfathers, John and Edwin.

> **The English and Anglo Colonials typically used maternal surnames as first names for their sons.**

About the mid-18th century, when middle names began to be popular; this practice was further expanded. Even daughters at this point commonly bore the father's or grandfather's first name, family surnames, or some other relatives' name as their first or middle names. For example: Ann *Currie* Miller; Mary *Samuel* Parsons; *Wilson Penrose* Evans; *Hunter Graham Archer* Jones; and Maria *Randolph Carter Ambler* Ruffin. Generally each name signifies part of the family tree, but not necessarily a direct line. It was not uncommon to name a younger child for a more distant (especially if prominent) relation. We found one child, for instance, named after his step-grandmother's first husband! Fortunately, the relationship is usually much closer; so when familes followed this practice, you may gain many helpful clues, (e.g., discovery of maternal lines) as you learn the complete names of all family members.

Names are sometimes difficult to uncover because the person may have been known only by his initials. This practice evidently derived from England, where even today it's popular. You may thus need to consult a family Bibles, or birth/christening records before discovering the names to which these initials refer.

While common use of surnames as Christian names, and a strong tendency to carry on traditional names generally provide us with good clues; yet, intermarriage between relatives, and using hero names to occasionally supplant family member names, sometimes results in complex, if not downright misleading, naming patterns. *George Washington*, *Patrick Henry*, and *Fayette* (and other forms of *Marquis Lafayette*) were popular hero-names of the Revolutionary era. President's names were also popular later on; or the namesake's hero might be a locally popular minister, the delivering midwife, or simply a good family friend. Therefore, look for substantiation when a particular line of descent is hypothesized on the basis of this surname=Christian name pattern.

While first names still provide some clues, they are less useful beginning about the mid-nineteenth century when popular, rather than family first names became more common.

SPELLING PROBLEMS AND HELPS

It has only been quite recently that even the lexicographers have agreed on spelling. Observe, e.g., how one word was spelled in four different, accepted dictionaries of the early 19th century: *creatshur*, *cretshure*, *creature*, and *creture*. And, as European names were spoken by the varying accents found in this country, different written variations naturally occurred. Thus, America truly was a *melting pot* when it came to spelling and pronunciation. In some families, each branch may have ended up with a pronunciation and spelling of their surname different from every other.

A typical example is provided by a Swiss immigrant ancestor of ours whose original Germanic name was **Bücher**. The following main spellings were found as we traced this family through the colonial and later eras were: *Boocher*, *Butcher*, *Boogher*, *Bugher*, *Bouer*, *Booher*, *Bougger*, *Boucher*, and *Booker*. And, occasionally, because of how closely the Germans pronouce **B** and **P**, it was also spelled with the initial **P**. While it was a relatively uncommon name, there were common Germanic names that produced variations close to it. We never knew, for instance, when coming across many *Bauers* in an index, whether (by a slip of the county clerk's pen, or the slurring of our ancestor's tongue) hidden among them may have been one of our family. Conversely, we did not automatically assume each *Bouer* found was a family member, but sought confirming evidence.

> We can't over-stress the importance of searching for all variant spellings of your family names. Probably more research fails because simple spelling precautions aren't taken, than for any other single reason.

The most helpful records, after all, do you no good if they are filed under *Unsmun* and *Eintsmen*, and you check only under the spelling *Heinzeman*. Here are suggestions and examples that should help:

o If the name began with a vowel or an **H**, look under every vowel, (including combinations, and substitutes): e.g.; *Argyle*, might also be spelled: *Ergoll Eargle, Eigle, Irgle, Urgull, Orgle, Oargel, Yargell* or *Jurgell*, while *Ackerman, Eckemman, Eickmann, Ikeman, Oeckerman*, or *Uckleman* may be variants of *Hackerman*.

o If your name starts with one or more consonant(s), first look for it under each different vowel following that consonant, e.g., *Branson, Brenson, Brinson, Bronson*, and *Brunson*. Extra letters may also have been inserted, such as *Brandtson, Bhrandsen, Berantsen, Brannison*. So to make sure no alternative form is overlooked, next look through every name beginning with the given consonant.

o Where prefixes may have been added or deleted, or when initial letters are close in sound to another letter, then obviously other initial letters will have to be considered. In the earlier *Cosgriff* example, three initial letters (**C**, **M**, and **O**) must be checked to recover all possible spelling variants. Locational prefixes such as *Van(der)*, (Dutch); *Le, La, De, Du*, (French); *Am, Zu*, and *Zum* (German); or *Da, Di, Dal, Del, Della*, (Italian); were sometimes retained, sometimes dropped, and sometimes changed.

MEANING CHANGES

The word *diskette* is not in older dictionaries, though now a common word. And the word *gay* will have quite a different meaning there than it has now. These examples show how living languages are in a state of constant flux. Mistakes do occur in using today's meanings to interpret yesterday's records. Here are some commonly misinterpreted terms:

In-law: Referred to all related by marriage, and therefore included relations we today refer to by the term *step-*. If your ancestor in a 1699 will names a *sonne-in-laue*, he may be referring to the man who married his daughter, or to his wife's son by a prior marriage. But if he names several son-in-laws with the same surname, we can probably correctly assume these are step-sons. Also note that a *father-in-law* or *mother-in-law*, in early colonial records, invariably refer to a step-parent; in our research we have not found what we now term "parent-in-laws" called anything except:

Loving. or well-beloved. friend(s): Common terms that usually, but not always, indicated some relationship.

Cousin: About five centuries ago served as a generic term for *relative*. The most common equivalent some two and half centuries ago was niece or nephew. Same meaning as today only within about the last one and a half centuries.

Niece/nephew: These are derived from the Latin terms for *granddaughter* and *grandson*, so in records going back several centuries, these meanings might be intended. In later records, however, they often have the same meaning we associate with them today. We have also seen *nephews* used generically, referring to both nieces and nephews.

Mrs.: An abbreviation of *mistress*; and was used to denote a woman of higher social class, rather than referring to her marital status, until the 18th century.

Junior/senior: Not necessarily related; these were common tags used to distinguish same-named contemporaries by their comparative ages. If more than two had the same name, they then might be designated as John Smith *Sr.*, John Smith *2nd*, John Smith *3rd*, etc., and each would move up one higher numerical niche when the next-older John Smith died or moved. Obviously, this could result in much confusion for one attempting to research among them.

My now wife: A legal term, often seen in will records. Rather than inferring that the man was married previously, it is used to protect himself in case of a future wife. (Because wills and land records, both important genealogical sources, often contain some difficult, legal terminology, you may frequently need to refer to the definitions given in Appendix E. In some cases you may need the further aid of a legal dictionary.)

Brother/sister: In early New England records sometimes refers to church friends, rather than to to actual siblings. (Each location you research may thus have its own idiosyncracies in terminology; this is some of the background you need to gain.)

AGE, TAX, AND GENDER REQUIREMENTS

English common law was followed by the colonies and most states (except those settled by the Spanish or French and based on community property: Arizona, California, Idaho, Louisiana, Nevada, New Mexico, Texas, and Washington). English common law distinguished two ages for legal activities. A younger age of limited rights, or *age of discretion*, was 12 for females; 14 for males. A *child of tender years* refers to one under this age. *Legal age*, or *adulthood* when full legal rights were enjoyed, was 18 for females; 21 for males (a *minor*, or *infant* being under this age).

Thus, a male orphan of age 13 had his guardian appointed by the court. But once age 14 was attained, he could choose his own guardian. So if you find among county records a dated entry in which your great grand-aunt requests her eldest brother (your great-grand father) to be her guardian, you can approximate both their ages. On this date she was between 12 and 18, while he was at least 21, the minimum age requirement for a guardian. Or, if you find a guardian record dated June, 1797, for your under-age male ancestor, and then find him on a jury, acting as a plaintiff in a trial, or writing a will bequeathing land during the month of March, 1798; you have proof of a birthdate between June, 1776 and March, 1777; as all those latter activities could only be done by someone of legal age.

The earliest guardian account also gives proof of, and makes it possible to approximate an otherwise unknown deathdate for a deceased parent. A *consent* found on a marriage record again allows ages to be approximated for the participant(s), as most states required a minor to present a written consent from the parent or guardian (these, therefore giving relationship evidence as well). All states required the bride and groom to have at least attained the age of discretion; some added 2-3 years more.

The age when males could be taxed varied, but was usually between 16 and 21. Learning tax legislation for a state you're researching may thus help you approximate ages. In Virginia a valuable research source from the late 18th century are county **tithable** (tax) lists. To interpret these, however, it helps to know that they listed first, the taxpayer, then male white family members over age 16, followed by any overseers or bound servants, and lastly slaves, male and female, over age 16. Between October, 1777, and May, 1783, the age requirement for charging sons as tithables was raised to 21, and on that last date county courts were given authority to take lists of free male tithables 16 through 21.

The status of women is another legality affecting your search. For most English-speaking countries, the farther back you go in time, the less likely you'll find maiden names. One list of marriage records we checked in Augusta Co., the parent-county of western Virginia and points westward, gives only the names of the grooms (presumably to save record-space). This was as late as the 1760's! Also, under common law, a married woman was unable to make a will, sell land, or otherwise dispose of her property (often, even when a marriage settlement stipulated otherwise). So no need to look for land or will records for a married woman until and unless she was subsequently widowed.

HANDWRITING

Handwriting is the source of direct and indirect problems. Because of similarity between the handwritten forms of *David* and *Daniel*, e.g., even in a typewritten index of handwritten records, the mistaken *David–Daniel* identity is still likely; check under both names. Much greater stumbling-blocks may arise from deciphering handwriting directly. But because handwriting differences evolved gradually, and if beginning research in the present and proceeding back gradually, you may not have encounter too much of a problem for many generations. The more ancient scripts can be quite difficult, however. Contact a local University language department for help with non-English scripts. And here are some additional helps:

o *From You to Your Ancestors* LDS Sunday School Manual, ($1.25; obtain from a local LDS Church library); short lesson for English script, 19th-17th centuries.

o *The Handwriting of American Records for a Period of 300 Years* by E. Kay Kirkham; Logan, UT: Everton Press; 3rd pr, 1981.

o *How to Read German Church Records without Knowing Much German* and *Spelling and Pronunciation of German Names* by Arta Johnson (153 Aldrich Rd., Columbus, OH 43214) *The Source* (see earlier); also has examples of early Germanic script.

There were other important differences besides changes in letter formation. An archaic letter, *ſ* , was equivalent to the double "s," and used through the 18th century. The little *punctuation* there was, was different. Dots to indicate pauses or stops may be the only marks. *Abbreviations*, on the other hand, are common. Not only were first names often shortened, but sometimes even surnames! Knowing this can help you deduce the abbreviation.

Jno or *Jno*, and *Jas* or *Ja^s*, for instance, were common abbreviations of *John* and *James*. But longer names may have been shortened many ways. *Christopher*, *Christian* and *Christianna* were often shortened by replacing *X* for the *Christ* part of the name: *X^{ofer}* or *X* , *X^n*, and *X^{ianna}*. (The last letters in abbreviations are often written as superscript.) *Do* or *d^o* are abbreviated forms of the commonly used *ditto*. And here are a few other abbreviations commonly found in original records or published genealogies:

ae. = age	MB = Marriage Book
bp./ch. = baptism/christening	OB = Order BOOK
bur. = burial	O.S. = Old Style (in Appendix C)
c. or ca. = circa (about)	s.a. = died unmarried
DB = deed Book	sic = correct copy
d.s.p. = died without children	twp. = township
d.y. = died young	ult. = in the past month
et al= and others	VB = Vestry Book
et ux = and wife	w.d. = will dated
inst. =in the present month	w.p. = will proved

SUMMARY

Care must be taken to ensure correct interpretation of original records. These examples will prove directly useful to many of you. Additionally, you will want to look out for similar kinds of possibilities whenever researching an unfamiliar place, time-period, or culture.

Chapter 15. CORRESPONDENCE AND ADDRESSES

PRODUCTIVE CORRESPONDENCE

One of today's great advantages is the ease and speed with which we can communicate with people, organizations, databases, and information centers (chapter 4 discussing modem-use to telecommunicate with these latter two). This is indeed fortunate because effective communication has the potential to advance your genealogy as much, or perhaps more than any other single factor. Although communicating well does not come naturally to most of us; but, just as in organizing data, following certain proven principles helps to ensure your success:

o Clearly define in your own mind the specific facts you want.

o Do enough research to learn who can most likely furnish those facts. Learn something about the organization first (services provided, fees charged, etc.)

o Don't ask others to gather or compile facts which you can do yourself.

o Observe the 6 *C*s in your letters:

* 1. Clean appearance
* 2. Clear expression
* 3. Concise wording
* 4. Convincing tone
* 5. Courteous style
* 6. Correct margins, spelling, grammar, etc.

o Keep your communications short and simple. Avoid form letters, but an easily-filled-out questionnaire (with blanks for your respondent to put in the answers) or a simple chart often helps. A known relative may enjoy family news besides your genealogical requests; otherwise, keep to the point (and certainly forego explaining your pedigree problems to overworked clerks!) Ask but one genealogical question at a time (especially the 1st time).

o Routinely request names and addresses of others who can help you.

o Send along a self-addressed, stamped envelope (SASE) except when dealing with organizations charging fees. Send sufficient money (use checks or money orders when writing to organizations) to cover any expense involved. Even relatives shouldn't be expected to give something for nothing. When not sure of charges, you can guess and/or offer to pay upon finding them out. Genealogists who enjoy good success in writing churches usually include a donation (e.g., "in memory of my _____ ancestors");

o Use titles for public officials (to avoid having your letter forwarded in case of transfer).

o When writing a foreign office, send at least two international postal reply coupons; use money order or bank drafts rather than cash; and write in the language of that country. (Research aids available from the GSU offer addresses and sample letters written to clerks in countries such as France, Germany, Italy, Poland, Romania, and Yugoslavia.) Expect long delays (often months, rather than weeks)! Remember to do your homework about this country first.

o Make copies of all letters and arrange as explained in Chapter 3.

o Be consistent for best results. A friend of ours has devoted an hour to genealogical correspondence and phone-calls each Sunday afternoon over a period of years. Needless to say, the results of such regular efforts are impressive.

HELPFUL ADDRESS SOURCES

Crockford's Clerical Directory. London: Oxford Univ. Press, biennial. (Church of England addresses.)

Deutsches Kirchliches Addressbuch, 3rd ed. Berlin, 1937. (Protestant Church addresses in Germany.)

Encyclopedia of Associations, 18th ed. Detroit: Gale Research Co., 1984. (International scope, but mostly American entries.)

The Official Catholic Directory. Annual. P.J. Kenedy and Sons: Skokie, IL.

Jacquet, Constant H., ed. *Yearbook of American and Canadian Churches*. Nashville and New York: Abingdon Press, 1974.

Directory: Historical Societies and Agencies in the United States and Canada, biennial. Nashville: American Association for State and Local History, 1983.

Record Repositories in Great Britain. London: Her Majesty's Stationery Office, 1973.

Suelflow, August R. A *Preliminary Guide to Church Records Repositories*. n.p.: Church Archives Committee, Society of American Archivists, 1969 (Addresses of USA Church repositories: lists services offered.)

Young, Margaret Labash, ed. *Directory of Special Libraries and Information Centers*, 8th ed. Detroit: Gale Research Co., 1974. (USA and Canada.)

American Library Directory. New York: RR Bowker, 1951-. (Addresses of USA libraries.)

Everton, George. *The Handy Book for Genealogists*, 8th ed., 4th pr., Logan, UT: Everton Publications, Inc., 1984. (Contains addresses of county clerks and state and local historical and genealogical societies, all arranged under state. Pertinent addresses for some other countries also included. Updates for society addresses and libraries are also found yearly in the July-August issue of *The Genealogical Helper*, put out by this same publisher.)

And don't forget *phonebooks*. Call the business office number found in the front of your phonebook to ask about out-of-state or foreign directories. For a nominal fee they can deliver to your door one for the very locality you are researching; relatives still living there may be well-worth writing or phoning. And, especially for less-common surnames, it may help while travelling to check local phonebooks as a means of locating scattered, living relatives.

ADDRESSES OF SOME LARGE AMERICAN GENEALOGICAL COLLECTION

We are including just some of the major USA library collection addresses; there are many more. If you can, use those in the area of your research interest, after first checking out those nearest to you. Addresses may change frequently; we cannot guarantee currency of all those found in this chapter, although we have checked out many).

Allen County Public Library
PO Box 2270
Fort Wayne , IN 46802; 219-424-7241
(Genealogical collection national in scope (including some Canada) with local emphasis on Indiana;
includes a set of USA federal census records and indexes . Staff will answer brief queries and
make photocopies for nominal charges , as well as recommend genealogists for Indiana .)

The American Antiquarian Society .
185 Salisbury St .
Worchester , Mass . 01609; 617-755-5221
(It is one of the largest of its kind in the country . National collection including Canada , of old
newspapers , city directories , printed genealogies , local histories , etc . Probably best utilized by
personal visit . No membership fee required; but stacks are closed and materials don't circulate .)

Burton Historical Collection , Detroit Public Library
5201 Woodward Ave .
Detroit , MI 48202
(Among the largest of USA collections; international in scope; complete for New England states ,
and probably largest in US for Ontario , Quebec , New York , New Jersey and Pennsylvania .)

BYU Genealogical Library
Room 4385 Harold B . Lee Library
Brigham Young University
Provo , Utah 84602; 801-378-3933
(Genealogical collection emphasizing local history in USA , England , Continental Europe ,
Scandinavia and Canada . Staff does quick-name-searches into some of their collections: DAR
Burial Lists; IGI; many USA Federal Censuses and indexes; early Mormon records; New York Times
Obituary Index; and Hamburg Direct Passenger Lists , 1855-1901 . Write for costs and details;
University also sponsers a well-done , reasonably-priced 4 day summer genealogy seminar .)

Genealogical Department
Library of Congress
Washington , DC 20504
(The Genealogy and Local History Collection is international in scope and open to adults . Most
stacks are closed , but well-used books are immediately available and service is quite good . Staff
answers brief queries . Catalogs of their family and local histories have been published and are
available at most libraries; see these listed in our Bibliography , Chapter 7).

Genealogical Library of the Church of Jesus Christ of Latter-day Saints
35 North West Temple Street
Salt Lake City , UT 84150; 801-531-2331
(Brand new building opened late 1985 . International collection of printed and microfilmed sources .
Stacks open Tues-Sat 7:30 a . m . -10 p . m .; Sat . 8-5; Mon . 7:30-6 . No charge; world-wide
branch system . (See Chapter 2 .)

The Huntington Library
San Marino , CA 91108
(Extensive , very valuable historical collections , including many early British and colonial USA .)

Maryland Historical Society
201 W . Monument St .
Baltimore , MD 21201; 301-685-3750
(National in scope but strongest for MD , PA , VA , and other eastern states . Open to public by
daily admission fee or by membership reading ticket . Most stacks open; brief inquiries will be
answered by the staff; will also supply a list of professional genealogists upon request .)

National Archives (GSA)
Pennsylvania Ave. at 8th St., NW
Washington, DC 20408; 202-655-4000
(Census, military, land records, passenger lists. Open to public; 8 branches (Appendix D.)

National Genealogical Society Library
1921 Sunderland Place, NW
Washington, DC 20036; 202-785-2123
(International collection with emphasis on U.S. Open to public with a charge for nonmembers. Books circulate to members only.)

National Society, Daughters of American Revolution (DAR) Library
1776 D Street, NW
Washington, DC 20006; 202-628-1776
(National in scope. One of best sources of local (county, city) records. Entire library has been designed for easy genealogical research. There is a charge for use of the library by nonmembers; closed to public in April.)

Newberry Library
60 West Walton St.
Chicago, IL 60610; 312-943-9090
(International collection: USA, emphasis on local history; Canada; British Isles; and Western Europe. At one point the largest American genealogical collection. Open to public; most stacks closed; collection is noncirculating.)

New England Historic Genealogical Society Library
101 Newbury St.
Boston, MA 02116; 617-536-5740
(New England and New York emphasis, but Canadian and British materials included. Open to public, nonmembers pay a daily fee. Members only have access to stacks, or may borrow books.)

New York Genealogical and Biographical Society
122-126 East 58th St
NYC, NY 10022; 212-755-8532
(National collection emphasizing New York City, New York, and Eastern states. Stacks open to members. Staff will answer a brief question, or provide genealogist list, if SASE included.)

New York Public Library
5th Ave and 42nd St.
NYC, NY 10016; 212-930-0828
(Local history emphasis for USA and Great Britain. The Local History and Genealogy Department is open to the public, but most stacks are closed. Staff won't answer questions, but will send list of genealogists if SASE included.)

Western Reserve Historical Society Library
10825 East Boulevard
Cleveland, OH 44106; 216-721-5722
(Emphasis upon Ohio, but includes family and local histories for USA and Canada. Open to public; but nonmembers must pay a daily fee. Staff will answer brief questions.)

LARGE GENEALOGICAL PUBLISHERS/BOOKSTORES IN USA

The Bookmark
PO Box 74
Knightstown, IN 46148

Tuttle Antiquarian Books, Inc.
PO Box 541
Rutland, VT 05701
(Out of print books; supplies.)

Genealogical Publishing Co. Inc.
1001 No. Calvert St.,
Baltimore, MD 21202
(Largest publisher: books, reprints.)

George K. Schweitzer
407 Regent Court
Knoxville, TN 37923
(*How-to* books for USA research.)

Jonathan Sheppard Books
Box 20201 ESP Station
Albany, NY 12220
(Includes good map collection
& search service for hard-to-find
locations in Europe & N. America

Hearthstone Bookshop
108 S. Columbus St
Alexandria, VA 22314
(Provide a valuable search
service for out-of-print books
$1.00 per title)

Ye Olde Genealogie Shoppe
PO Box 39128
Indianapolis, IN 46239
(Books, supplies, research
& "Midwestern Genealogy")

Goodspeed's Book Shop, Inc.
7 Beacon St.
Boston, Mass. 02108

Closson Press
1935 Sampson Dr
Apollo, PA 15613-9738
(Books, supplies; specialize in PA)

Everton Publishers, Inc.
PO Box 368
Logan, UT 84321
(Largest magazine; supplies/books/research.)

Southern Historical Press
PO Box 738
Easley, SC 29640
(Publishes *Georgia Genealogical Magazine*)

University Microfilms, Inc.
300 North Zeeb Road
Ann Arbor, Michigan 48106
(To locate a book/article, obtain copyright
clearance if necessary, & xerox. Expensive
but a needed service. SASE for forms.)

Ancestry, Inc
POB 476
SLC, UT 84110
(A major publisher, services, newsletter,
book-club, and buyers guide.)

FOREIGN ADDRESSES

Some addresses have been corrected and many added since our last edition, thanks to several people named in the "Acknowledgements" section. The GSU research aids, as previously mentioned, also provide good help for many countries. U.S. Embassy officers in each country can often help to obtain offical reords; contact them as needed.

(While the next several pages represent a large percent of the pertinent foreign addresses, yet this section is obviously incomplete for many of the countries. We cordially invite those with additional pertinent information to share that with us prior to our next revision.)

AFRICA

Write the consulate general of the desired country. Most of these are located in Washington, DC, and New York. Phone books (often found in public libraries) have addresses, or request through directory assistance; i.e. 212-555-1212 for New York, and 202-555-1212 for DC.

NORTH and SOUTH AMERICA--excluding the United States

CANADA: Public Archives of Canada, 395 Wellington St., Ottawa, Ontario K1A ON3 will send free a booklet: *Tracing Your Ancestors In Canada*; it lists each provincial *Archive*.

CUBA: Cuban Refugee Emergency Center, 747 Ponce de Leon Blvd., Coral Gables, FL 33134

MEXICO : Archivo General de la Nacion, Palacio Nacional, Mexico City, 2, D.R.

CENTRAL and EAST EUROPE (Including IRON CURTAIN ADDRESSES)

ALBANIA: Roman Catholic and Orthodox Churches kept parish records until 1929 when civil registration began; birth marriage and death records were then kept by local municipality officers. Records are maintained in the Prime Minister's Office, but officials are uncooperative and don't generally make them available to researchers.

AUSTRIA : Austrian National Tourist Office, 545 5th Ave., NYC, NY 10017. Provincial archives are found in the city or town as follows (and church records for the province are from the date found in parentheses): Burgenland in Eisenstadt (1896-1921); Carinthia in Klagenfurt (1840); Lower Austria in Vienna (1817); Styria in Groz (1835); Tyrol in Innsbruck (1816); Upper Austria in Salsburg and Linz (1817); and Voralberg in Bregenz. Vienna City Districts 1-9 (1812) and City Districts 10-26 (1797) are all in Vienna.

BALTIC STATES as follows: in *ESTONIA*, registrars of Towns or in the relevant courts, such as probate or land; in *LATVIA*, District Court in Riga, Jelgava, Liepaja, or Daugavpils State Archives for records over 10 years old; in *LITHUANIA*, at Central State Archives, or at the offices of Notaries Public (formerly Justices of the Peace), and in District Courts.

BULGARIA: Bulgarian Tourist Office, 161 E. 86th ST., NYC, NY 10028. Generally uncooperative. They have records from 1893 in the District People's Councils. The Ministry of Justice has old records; Court of Justice has new records; Notary Public also has some records.

CZECHOSLOVAKIA: Czechoslovak Travel Bureau, 10 E. 40th St., NYC, NY 10016. Consular Division of Czechoslovak Soc. Republic; 3900 Linnean Ave. NW; Washington, DC 20008 will search Czeck records for a $30 or up minimum fee; we know of several who have had good results using this service. You may also address inquiries to: Archivai Sprava; Prague 6, Tride o Brancu miru 133; or Slovenaska Archivni Sprava, Bratislava, Vajanskeho; Nabrezit. The Czech Heritage Society of Texas has begun a series. Volume 1 identifies over 6,300 Czech immigrants who came to America through the ports of Galveston, New Orleans, New York and Baltimore before 1880. $15.96; order through Leo Baca, 1707 Woodcreek, Richardson, TX 76081.

GERMANY: German National Tourist Office, 747 3rd Ave., NYC, NY 10017. For vital records, address letter to: Standesamt (Civil Registry Office) in place where the event occurred. Verlag Degener & Co.; Postfach 1340, D8530 Neustadt/Aisch, W. Germany will translate queries and publish them in several German genealogical periodicals (about $15-20 for a moderately long query; send a dollar with query for exact cost); also have genealogical and local history books; write for a listing, specifying interests. Heimatstelle Pfalz; Benzinoring 6; D-6750 Kaiserslautern, W.

Germany will check their files; send facts on your immigrant German ancestor with 3 International Postal reply coupons. The NGS has a list of 25 Genealogical Societies in Germany including one or more in: Baden-Wurttenberg; Bayern; Berlin; Bremen; Franken; Hamburg; Hessen, Mitteldeutschland; Niedersachsen; Oldenburg; Ostdeutschland; Ostrfriesland; Ost-Und Westpreuben, Pfalz; Rheinland; Saarland; Schleswig-Holstein; and Wastfalen.

GREECE: Greek National Tourist Organization, 645 5th Ave., NYC, NY 10022. Birth records kept in each community since 19th century. Municipality archives have records back to the 16th century for some (mostly noble) families.

HUNGARY: Hungarian Travel Bureau; 630 5th Ave., NYC, NY 10111. Civil registration (births, marriages, deaths) have been kept since October, 1895 and are in the National Center of Archives, Leveltarak Orszagos Kozpontja, Budapest 1, Uri Utca 54-56. There is also a Library associated with the Hungarian National Archives: Magyar Orszagos Levettar Konyvtara, Budapest 1, Becsikaputer 4. Baptismal records, kept as early as 1515, are also in these National Archives, or else the Central Economic Archives (also in Budapest), or the Provincial Archives of the various provinces. Write the Information Officer of the Hungarian Embassy.

POLAND: Tourist Office, 500 5th Ave. NYC, NY 10036. An Ancestor Index Card file (people researching Polish familes) is in the Polish Museum of America; c/o Polish Genealogical Society, 984 N. Milwaukee Ave. Chicago, IL 60622. Send SASE. Polish Nobility Association, Villa Anneslie, 529 Dunkirk Road, Anneslie, MD 21212 has a library and newsletter. The Catholic Church books for Polish (but formerly German) provinces are stored at: Bischoefliche 2 Entralarchiv D 8400, Regensburg, St. Petersweg II, West Germany. Biuro Heraldyke Polskie (Polish Heraldry Bureau); 58-560 Jelenia Gora Zdroj; Skrytka Pocztowa 73. This is Poland's first company specializing in family research. Set up by a Polish nobleman, it is fully licensed by the Polish authorities. Free initial consultation; send in surname, mother's maiden name and grandparent's names. (American embassy in Warsaw will also obtain records for a slight charge.) Old records in Polish National Archives: Ul Dluga 6 Skr. Poczt 1004 00-950; Warsaw.

ROMANIA: Romanian National Tourist Office, 573 3rd Ave., NYC, NY 10016.

RUSSIA: Russian Travel Bureau, 20 E. 46th St., NYC, NY 10017. Another source of help is the Russian Genealogical Society, 971 1st Ave., NYC, NY 10022. Russia is uncooperative to researchers. Nicholas Ikonnikor, President of le Bureau de Genealogique, Union de la Noblesse Russe (8 Rue Gabrielle d/Estrees, Vannes, Seine, France) has 20 volumes on Russian families.

YUGOSLAVIA: Yugoslav National Tourist Office, 630 5th Ave., NYC, NY 10111. Croatian-Servian-Slovene Genealogical Society; 2527 San Carlos Ave., San Carlos, CA 94070 has library and newsletter. Archiv Bosne I Hercegovine, Sarajevo, Save Kovacevica 6, Bosnia. And some records available via the Lawyer's Association: Udruzenje Pravnika FNRJ; Belgrade, Proleterskit; Brigada 74.

FAR EAST

CHINA : Research almost requires a visit. But ancestral information is available from each district cemetery, family temple and ancestral hall, and these can be contacted by mail.

JAPAN. National Diet Library, 1-10-1 Nagata-cho, Chivoda-ku, Tokyo 100.

PHILIPPINES. General Services Department, Records Management Bureau, San Luis Street, Manila.

MID-EAST

ISRAEL: Free booklet, *Tracing Your Jewish Roots,* from Rabbi Malcolm Stern, American Jewish Archives, 3101 Clifton Ave., Cincinnati, OH 45220. Also in this country: American Jewish Committee, 165 E. 56th St., NYC, NY 10022 (publishes year book); American Jewish Historical Society, 3080 Broadway, NYC, NY 10027; Yivo Institute for Jewish Research, 1048 5th Ave., NYC, NY 10028; American Jewish Historical Society, 2 Thornton Road, Waltham, MA 02154. For recent Israeli Jewish family origins write to any of the following: Institute for Research or Jewish Families, Tel Aviv; Yad Vashem, Remembrance Authority, PO Box 84, Jerusalem Disapora Research Institute, Tel Aviv University, Tamat–Aviv, Israel; Institute for Contemporary Jewery, and/or Central Jewish Archives; Hebrew University, Givat Tam, Jerusalem; and Yad Vishem Museum Archive, PO Box 3477, Jerusalem.

MISCELLANEOUS

ALDERNEY: Registrar General's Office (for Wills); Registrar to Ecclesiastical Court (for Vita Records). Address: 9 Lefebre St., St Peter Port, Gurnsey.

ICELAND. Parish National Archives in Reykajavik have records from 1745 to present.

ISLE OF MAN & CHANNEL ISLANDS : Registrar General, government Office in Wonglas have records from 1849.

SCANDINAVIA

DENMARK : Danish Tourist Board, 75 Rockefeller Plaza, NYC, NY 10019. Records from 1863 in the Danish State Archives Dept., Public Record Office in Copenhagen, Zealand, and Lolland Falster. Regional Archives, Landsarkivet, 10 Jagtvej, DK 2200, Copenhagen N.

FINLAND. Finland National Tourist OFfice, 75 Rockefeller Plaza, NYC, NY 10019. Records date from 1540 in the Central Archives of Helsinki. Those written in Finnish found in: Valtionarkioto, Rauhankater 17, Helsinki; those written in Swedish: Riksarkivet, Fredsgatan 17, Helsingfors. Estate inventories (Boupptechningar) are in Town Archives; Finnish records are also available in London and New York libraries. Two genealogical organizations may also help: Geneaiogiska Sumfundet i Finland, Snellmansgatan 9–11, Helsinki; and Helsingfors Slaktforsakare R. F., C/ N. Nock, Kentelevagen 42, SF–00320 Helsingfors.

NORWAY : Free booklets: *Norwegian Ancestors* from the National Tourist office, 75 Rockefeller Plaza, NYC, NY 10019; & *How to Trace Your Ancestors in Norway* from the Royal Norwegian Ministry of Foreign Affairs, Office of Cultural Relations, Mossevn 40, Oslo. Supreme Lodge of Sons of Norway, 1312 West Lake St., Minneapolis, MN. Norsk Sledtshistorisk Forening, Ovre Slottsgate 17, Oslo. Records since 1700 at the Central Bureau of Statistics. The Chief Demographic Section, Statistisk, Sentralyra, Dronningans Gate 16, Oslo. National Archives, Riskarkivet, Banpplass 3, Oslo. Regional State Archives (Statsarkivet) addresses are as follows Bergen, Arstadveien 32; Hamar, Stadgaten 71; Kristiansand, Veoterveien 4; Oslo, Kirkegaten 14- 18; Stenanger, Peder Klows Gate 27; Tromso, Petersborg Gate 21–29; Trondheim, Hogskoleveien 12.

SWEDEN. Free booklets: *Americans from Sweden* (Swedish Embassy, Watergate 600, 600 New Hampshire Ave. NW, Washington DC 10037) & *Tracing Your Swedish Ancestry* (Royal Swedish Ministry of Foreign Affairs, Stockholm. National Archives: Riksarkinet, Arkingatan 4 Stockholm)

WESTERN EUROPE

BELGIUM. Belgium National Tourist Office, 745 5th Ave., NYC, NY 1002? M. E. Sabbe, L'Archiviste General, Archives Generalaes du Royaume, 78 Galarie Ravenstein, Brussels. State Archive locations: Antwerp: 5 Door-Verstraeteplaats; Arlon: Place Leopold; Bruges: 14–18 Akademiestraat; Ghent: Geeraard Duivelstien; Hasselt: Bampslaan; Liege: 8 Rue Ponpllin; Mons: 23 Place du Park; Namur: 45 Rue d'Arguet. Also: Service de Centralisation des Etudes Genealogiques et Demographiques de Belgique, Secretary M.P.E. Claessens, 26 Rue Aux Gaines, Brussels. *Le Parchemin* a magazine that will print genealogical queries: Le Chevalier Zavier de Ghelline, L'Office Genealogique et Vaernewyk, Heraldique de Belgique, 37 rue Besquet, Brussels.

ENGLAND. British Tourist Authority, 680 5th Ave., NYC, NY 10019, or Plaza of the Americas, North Tower, Suite 750, LB 346, Dallas, TX 75201. International Society for British Genealogy, Box 20425, Cleveland, OH 44120. The Registrar-General, St. Catherine's House, 10 Kingsway, London, England WC2 6JP has post-1837 births, deaths, marriages; post-1858 wills; post-1881 censuses. Society of Genealogists, 14 Charterhouse Buildings, London EC1M 7BA (Phone 01-25 8799); Federation of Family History Societies of the U.K, c/o Colin R. Chapman, Gen. Secretary, The Dovers, Cambridge, Gloucester, England GL 2 7AN; or to Publications Dep't., c/o 96 Beaumont St., Milehouse Plymouth, PL2 3AQ to request list of member societies and periodicals; include SASE and 3 International Reply coupons, or equivalent U.K. stamps. British Museum Librarian, Bloomsbury, London, WC1 has records from 1759.

FRANCE. French Government Tourist Office, 610 5th Ave., NYC, NY 10020. Documentation Francaise, 29–31 quai Voltaire, 75340 Paris CEDEX 07. Town halls have kept vital records, but some towns have transferred their records to the departmental archives, which also have indexes for notarial records (with marriage contracts, estate records and deeds) dating from about 1700.

IRELAND. Irish Tourist Board, 590 5th Ave., NYC, NY 10036. The National Library, and Genealogical Office, Kildare St., Dublin 2, Ireland has largest collection. Call before visiting to see if a *ticket* is needed. Genealogical Office is mostly for advanced researchers, but offers advice to all library visitors, and has researchers available for research in all Dublin collections at an hourly fee. Before writing them see the books they have authored, especially *Handbook On Irish Genealogy*. Irish Genealogical Research Society, The Challanor Club, 59/61 Pont, London SW1, England has a library where research for a fee is available. Registry of Deeds at Henrietta St., Dublin 1. Deed copies about 1.6 Irish lbs. via airmail. First obtain deed numbers via indexes (which are also at the GSU). Public Record Office of No. Ireland (and the Ulster Historical Foundation [UHF] also at same address): 66 Balmoral Ave; Belfast BT1 5GD, No. Ireland. The UHF searches No. Ireland records; minimum fee about $20. Public Record Office, Four Courts, Dublin has 300,000 wills (dating as early as 1536); censuses; list of parish registers. Register General, General Register Office, Fermanagh House, Ormean Ave., Belfast has surviving births, marriages, deaths 1864–1921; Register-General, General Register Office, Joyce House, 8/11 Lombard St. East, Dublin 2 (Phone 01-71 1000) has birth, marriage, death records since 1921. Certificate cost, including search fees = 3 Irish pounds; photocopy of a specified entry = 1.5 Irish pounds. 6 hour general search = 10 Irish pounds. Add a dollar for postage. (Ask a bank to get current value of Irish pound; USA checks are acceptable.)

ITALY. Italian Government Tourist Office, 630 5th Ave., NYC, NY 10111. Very complete records; contact the archive closest to the town of origin: Instituto di Genealogia e Araldico, Via Antonio Cerasi 5-A, Roma; Instituto Araldico Coccia, Borgo Santa Croce 6, 50122 Firenze; Studio Araldico Scorza, Via Caffaro 3, 16124 Genova; Araldi Instituto Genealogico Italiano, Largo Chigi 19, 00187 Roma.

LUXEMBOURG. Luxembourg National Tourist Office, 801 2nd Ave., NYC, NY 10017. Their Public Rcords Office has records from 1793. Also: Archiviste de la Ville de Luxembourg, Hotel de Ville, Place Guillaume, Luxembourg.

MONACO. Monaco Government Tourist Bureau, 845 Third Ave., 2nd Floor, NYC, NY 10022.

NETHERLANDS. Netherlands National Tourist Office, 576 5th Ave., NYC, NY 10036. Central Bureau voor Genealogie, 18 Nasoanlaan, The Hague; Netherlands Genealogische Vereniging, PO Box 976, Amsterdam; and Royal Society for Genealogy and Heraldry, Konenklyk Nederlandsh Genoolschep voor Geslact in Wapenkunde, 5 Bleijenburg, The Hague.

PORTUGAL: Portuguese National Tourist Office, 548 5th Ave., NYC, NY 10036. All state records published in notary records; write to: Direccao Geral do Registoe Notariado, do Ministerio da Justica, Lisbon. For Parish Registers: The Director, Arquivo dos Registos Paroquinis dos Pruzeres, Lisbon, Portugal.

SCOTLAND. Central Reference Collection, Highland Region, Inverness Branch Library, Farraline Park, Inverness is a source of highland genealogical references. Central Library, George 1V Bridge, Edinburgh, Scotland EH1 1EG, has large Scottish family history collection. Scots Ancestry Research Service, 20 York Place, Edinburgh EH1 3EP. Public Records Office, Ruskin Ave., Kew, Richmond, Surrey TW9 4DU. General-Registry Office of Births, Marriages, Deaths, East end of Princess St., Edinburgh EH1 3YT has records from 1855.

SPAIN : Spanish National Tourist Office, 4800 The Galleria, 5085 Westheimer, Suite 4800, Houston, TX 77056. Instituto International de Genalogia y Heraldicer, A Partado de Correas., 7.077 Madrid; and National Historical Archives, Madrid.

SAMPLE LETTERS to a County Clerk, Relative. and Librarian

March 15, 1986

York County Clerk
Yorktown, VA 23490

Dear Sir,

My ancestor ROBERT READE was a resident of your county; according to Torrence's Virginia Wills and Administrations, 1632-1800, he left a will there dated 1798. I have included a check for $3 to have that will photocopied. Please inform me if any balance is due.

I thank you in advance for your help.

Sincerely,

Mr. Charles Wilson
1234 Bowling Green
Ottumwa, KS 56789

Dear Mr. Wilson,

Your name was given me by our relative Jeremy Grant. In a recent conversation he said you had a family record about our common ancestor Albert Humphreys. Being quite interested in our family history, I would very much appreciate having a copy of that record. $3 is included for photocopy costs. If insufficient, I'll be happy to pay any balance.

I am so pleased to learn about a relative with information about this branch of the family, and am hopeful we can become better acquainted, even if only by letter.

Sincerely,

April 23, 1986

Reference Librarian
Sassafrass Co. Public Library
Hard Rock, KS 55555

Dear Librarian,

My ancestors CYRUS BROWN and MARY FUNK were early residents in Sassafrass County; I would very much appreciate your checking for their names in any local history or other indexes your library might have, and also in the following book:

Bigler, Jacob. HARD ROCK VITAL RECORDS, 1977.

For any references found, please make photocopies and send them in the enclosed self-addressed stamped envelope. Enclosed is a check for $3.00; please advise if this is insufficient. (No need to check the following, as I have already: HISTORY OF SASSAFRASS COUNTY, 1948.)

Many thanks in advance for any help you can provide. Feel free to add comments, or names and addresses of others who might have helpful information, to this letter.

Yours truly,

A NOTE RE: WRITING COUNTY CLERKS

Microfilming of courthouse records during the past several decades has been a great help to researchers. But difficulties are typically encountered when trying through correspondence to obtain the as yet unmicrofilmed original records in county clerk's offices. There are, of course, some extra-helpful county clerks. If fortunate enough to deal with one, you'll certainly want to show appreciation; sending a letter of praise to the local paper when re-election time approaches, for example, may help both of you, as you would certainly benefit by retaining that clerk in office!

It is more common, however, for clerks to regard genealogists in the same category as some of the lower life-forms. Family history requests in some offices are routinely returned after a *no information found* stamp has been truthfully applied (no information was found, because none was sought!). Other clerks have been known to send genealogy requests straight to their "circular file" (maybe, or maybe not, removing any checks first). Remember, however, that reasons mostly beyond clerical control have contributed to this less-than-idyllic situation. Counties often overwork and underpay their staff; and clerks are rightfully irritated by genealogists who ask for too much, request records they don't have, or who aren't specific or clear in their requests.

Being aware that county clerks generally will not go out of their way to fulfill your fondest genealogical hopes, however, is not cause to surrender before even going to battle. Rather, it should encourage you to take steps to improve your chances of success: First, of course, do as much as you can without them. Most counties have had their indexes, and even some original records themselves, microfilmed by the GSU. Make full use of these, then, before contacting them for whatever else is needed. Next, study the geographical and jurisdictional background, including close examination of the *Handy Book*, to be sure of writing the correct place for the desired records. Lastly, having studied the published sources and microfilmed indexes, you will be able to provide specific names and dates. Precise description of the desired record to the county clerk (as in the York Co. letter) simplifies their search, and thus your likelihood of obtaining what is wanted.

Yet, in some cases, the county clerk may still fail to respond to your request. If too impatient to wait and try again under a later, hopefully more cooperative, clerk (or to go into politics yourself!); you will either have to arrange for a personal courthouse visit, or hire a genealogist in that locale to do your needed search (see next). Because county records so often play a crucial role in genealogical research, we look forward to the time when local courthouses begin making greater use of the technological advances in information storage and retrieval. This would help our counties greatly reduce both their space and financial (your tax) requirements, as well as make it possible to eliminate much of the hassle now typically connected with obtaining these records.

LISTS OF PROFESSIONAL RESEARCHERS

Another group of addresses that may be needed are those of genealogical researchers. Many (but not all) local and historical societies and libraries will supply the names of those who research the local records if you so request.

Probably the best of all these kinds of lists is the *List of Persons Certified* supplied by the National Genealogical Society. This fine, non-profit organization does a great work in testing and certifying genealogical competency. Specify in which of these areas you want to hire a certified researcher: *Certified Genealogist, Genealogical Record Searcher, American Lineage Specialist*(for patriotic societies); *American Indian Lineage Specialist, Genealogical Lecturer*, or *Genealogical Instructor*. A current list costs $2.00 and can be obtained from this address: Board of Certification of Genealogists, Box 19165, Washington, DC 20036.

A list of genealogists who have passed an accreditation examination administered by the Genealogical Department of The Church of Jesus Christ of Latter-Day Saints (i.e., have demonstrated competency to research in their library) may be obtained free from the GSU (50 North West Temple St., Salt Lake City, UT 84150, and include a SASE) or one of its branches.

SUMMARY

We trust these address listings and sample letters have started ideas flowing on how you may personally take advantage of correspondence and other forms of communication to advance your research. Communicating effectively with those people and organizations able to provide you desired information should substantially increase your success.

APPENDIX A. RESEARCH PROCEDURE DIAGRAM

#1. Search for and compile home sources: Bibles, letters, diaries, photos, documents, etc. Interview family; especially older relatives.

#2. Put facts onto charts. Begin with present generation, moving back one at a time. Document source of each fact separately.

#3A. Choose a line to research.

#3B. Check LDS library and compiled sources: what has been done?

#4. Evaluate obtained facts.

#5. Complete your records with proven facts; then begin research by assembling the specific names, dates, places known.

#6A. Set goals and plan research.

#6B. Obtain history/geography background, & facts about these records:

1. government vital
2. church
3. cemetery
4. probate
5. land
6. other court
7. census
8. military
9. migration/naturalization
10. others. . .

#6C. Locate these records

#6D. Search them; take notes/photocopy and interpret data

#6E. Analyze facts obtained; complete records or set new goals

#7. Write up research when still fresh in mind; what done, why, what found, and implications for further research. You can later expand this to publish or otherwise share with others.

RESEARCH PROCEDURE DIAGRAM: STEP-BY-STEP GENEALOGY

APPENDIX B. SUBJECT HEADING CHECKLIST

Use the following subject headings in your library research. GSU stands for the Genealogical Society of Utah; check these headings when using their collection. LC stands for Library of Congress; many libraries use that system. If not otherwise indicated, then the subject heading as given is used by both.

Archive Collections
Bible Records:See "Vital Records"
            (GSU); "Family Records" (LC)
Birth Records:See Vital Records
Cemetaries: See Vital Records (GSU)
Church History
City Directories:See"Directories"
City Histories: See "History"
Civil Records:See "Court Records" (LC)
County Histories: See "History"
Death Records: See "Vital Records"
Family Histories: under surname
Genealogy
Ghost Towns:See "History," "Geography"
            (GSU);"Cities & Towns, Ruined,
      Extinct," etc. (LC)
Historical Societies: See "Societies"
Land Ownership Maps
Maps
Marriage Records: See "Vital Records"
      (GSU); "Marriage Licenses" (LC)
Minorities
Mortality Schedules: See "Vital Rec-
      ords" (GSU); "Genealogy--Sources";
      "Census, (year)"; "Mortality" (LC)
Naturalization: See "Emigration and
      Immigration" (GSU)
Oral History
Periodicals
Plot Book: See "Land & Property--Maps"
      (GSU) "Real Property--Maps" (LC)
Post Offices: See "Postal Guides"
            (GSU); "Postal Service" (LC)
School Records: See "Schools"
Surnames: See "Names, Personal"
Tax Records: See "Taxation"
Voter Lists: See "Electorate"
            (GSU); "Voting Registers" (LC)

Atlases
Bibliographies
Biography
Boundaries
Census Schedules See: Census
Church Membership and Minutes See: "Church
      Records" (GSU); "Church Records and
      Registers" (LC)
County Atlases
Criminal Court Records See: "Court Records"
Emigration Records
Gazetteers
Geographical Names: See "Names,
      Geographical"
Historical Atlasses: See "Atlasses" (GSU);
      "Historical Geography--, Maps" (LC)
Immigration Records
Land Records: See "Land & Property" (GSU);
      "Deeds," "Land Titles"(LC)
Military History: See "Military Records"
      (GSU), "History, Military"; "Regimental
      Histories"; "History- -Registers, Lists,"
      etc.; --"Registers of Dead" (LC)
Mortuary Records: See "Vital Records"
      (GSU); "Mortality" (LC)
Newspapers
Patriotic Societies: See "Societies" (GSU)
Place Names: See Geographical Names
Poll Tax Lists: See "Electorate" (GSU);
      "Poll--Tax" (LC)
Probates: See "Probate Records"
Public Land: See "Land and Property" (GSU)
Ship Passenger Lists: See Emigrations and
      Immigratioin
Vital Records: See "Electorate" (GSU);
      "Voting Registers" (LC)
Wills: See "Probates"

APPENDIX C. 1752 CALENDAR CHANGE

In 1752 Britain, except Scotland (who made this change more than a century earlier) and her colonies switched from the Julian to the Gregorian calendar. Three changes resulted. First, a total of 11 days were added, so people born before, and still living after 1752, may have added 11 days to their birthdate. That is the reason George Washington's birthday, for instance, is designated as Feb. 22, even though actually he was born Feb. 11, 1732.

A second change, genealogically insignificant, was the introduction of leap year. The third change has proven most significant for researchers: changing new year's day from March 25 to Jan. 1. Because this change was anticipated for sometime before implementation, dates that therefore fell between January 1 and March 25 in years prior to 1752 were often written in a "double-dating" fashion, as, for example: *23 Mar 1729/30* , or *16 Jan 1750-1*. In such a notation, the earlier year is in reference to the calendar system then in use; the latter refers to the year as it would be under the soon-to-be-accepted, modern calendar system.

When the double-dating system was not used, a genealogist recording the uncorrected date may make mistakes. For example, a child's birthdate of 9 March 1747, compared to the parent's marriage date of 9 April 1747, could lead to the mistaken conclusion that the child was illegitimately born. When allowance is made for the calendar change, however, it is seen that the birth occurred 11 months following the marriage. Or, if you find a will dated September, 1680, and proved in February 1680, you will realize this is not the inpossibility it might otherwise appear to be.

Also, because the old style year began in March, this made a difference of two (months) in the month's numerical order. Overlooking this fact may again lead to dating mistakes, as months were often written or referred to numerically. September, for example, was the seventh month on the old style calendar, and often abbreviated "7-ber;" while, after the change, it became the ninth month.

APPENDIX D. NATIONAL ARCHIVES' REGIONAL BRANCHES

Atlanta *FARC
1557 St. Joseph Ave.
East Point, GA 30344

Boston *FARC
380 Trapelo Road
Waltham, MA 02154

Chicago *FARC
7358 South Pulaski Rd
Chicago, IL 60629

San Francisco *FARC
1000 Commodore Dr
San Bruno, CA 94066

New York *FARC
Bldg 22--MOT Bayonne
Bayonne, NJ 07002

Fort Worth *FARC
4900 Hemphill St.
PO Box 6216
Fort Worth, TX 76115

Los Angeles *FARC
24000 Avila Road
Laguna Niguel, CA 92677

Seattle *FARC
6125 Sand Point Way NE
Seattle, WA 98115

Philadelphia *FARC
5000 Wissahickon Ave.
Philadelphia, PA 19144

Denver *FARC
Bldg 48, Denver Federal Center
Denver, CO 80225

Kansas City *FARC
2306 East Bannister Road
Kansas City, MO 64131

(*FARC = Federal Archives and Records Centers.)

APPENDIX E. LEGAL TERMS from WILL, LAND, COURT RECORDS

o *Administration (Administrator/Administratrix)*: This is a process involving the collecting, managing, and distributing of an estate. When the person responsible for this process is chosen by the court (as happens when the decedent didn't leave a will, or when the person chosen as the *Executor* (q.v.) declines to accept), that person is known as the *Administrator* (if male) or *Administratrix* (if female.) Normally he or she must enter into a bond with sureties; note that the names of those bondsmen are often relations.

o *Affinity*: A connection through marriage, rather than through blood.

o *Age of Discretion*: Between 12 and 18 for females; between 14 and 21 for males under the old English *Common Law*.

o *Antenupital Agreement*: A contract made by a bride and groom-to-be setting forth their property rights. Usually (not always) made before second marriages to protect property of earlier children; most common among Dutch in New Netherland, and in *community property* states.

o *Attorney*: Anyone authorized to act on behalf of another. *Power of Attorney* is the document giving that authority.

o *Beneficiary*: Usually refers to those receiving by will, but can be anyone that a trust is created for, or receives a property benefit.

o *Bequeath (Bequest)*: The verb used when personal property is given by will. The noun refers to that personal property gift.

o *By these Presents*: Reference to the document in which it occurs.

o *Chattel*: Includes animate, as well as inanimate personal property; sometimes used as a synonym for slaves in earlier times.

o *Child of Tender Years*: Under age of discretion (q.v.).

o *Community Property*: Applies in Arizona, California, Idaho, Louisiana, Nevada, New Mexico, Texas, and Washington. All property obtained by either spouse during marriage is considered owned by them in common.

o *Consanguinity*: Blood relationship.

o *Consideration*: The price (or other motive) in a contract.

o *Corporeal (Incorporeal) Property*: Seeable property (e.g. a house) is corporeal. Unseen property (e.g. rent) is incorporeal.

o *Cotenancy*: Consists of joint ownership, of which there are four types:
   Community property--see above.
   Tenancy by the entirety--joint land ownership by spouses with rights of survivorship. Most states no longer allow this, unless specifically created in a legal document.
   Joint tenancy--like the above, but not limited to spouses, and can be terminated whenever any of the parties sells.
   Tenancy in common--concurrent land ownership by separate titles. No rights of survivorship, and can be terminated by any party.

o *Court of Probate* (also named *Circuit Court, Orphans' Court, Court of the Ordinary, Surrogate Court, District* or *County Court*, etc.): The court having jurisdiction of probate matters.

o *Curtesy*: The estate a man is entitled to upon the death of his wife in common law states.

o *Decedent*: A deceased person.

o *Deed* (or *Conveyance*) The document transferring title in real property. The most common kinds are the *deed in fee* (or simply *deed*) and *warranty deed*. Others are *quitclaim deeds, trust deeds, deeds of release, deeds of partition*, and *gift deeds*.

o *Deposition*: Written testimony, taken under oath.

o *Devise (Devisee/Devisor)*: A *devisor* is one who gives his real property (*devise*) by will to a devisee.

o *Dower (Endowment)*: Property to which a widow has claim under common law from her husband's estate (traditionally, 1/3). Setting off, or assigning, her dower is referred to as an *endowment*.

o *Escheat*: Property reversion to the state when no heirs are qualified.

o *Et Uxor*: Latin term meaning "and wife," often abbreviated *et ux*.

o *Executor/Executrix.* The person appointed by the *testator* (q.v.) to carry out will provisions.

o *Fee Simple.* A legal term referring to total ownership.

o *Folio.* A leaf, as in a book. In older records may refer to both sides of a leaf (i.e., 2 pages) or occasionally will refer to even more pages.

o *Guardian.* The person assigned the responsibility to care for another person's rights and property. Can be chosen ("elected") by a child who is over *age of discretion,* else, appointed by the court. A guardian (often the mother or step-mother) was commonly named when only the father was deceased. Less commonly, a father may be appointed guardian to his own child, e.g., when he is made trustee for property the child has inherited from a maternal grandparent.

o *Heir.* One who inherits from the death of another (usually an ancestor).

o *Indenture.* Reciprocal agreement signed by both parties. Many colonial immigrants came as *indentured servants,* meaning their passage was paid by, and other benefits received from, a master whom they agreed to serve for a stated period (e.g., 7 years).

o *Infant.* A minor; of less than legal age (q.v.).

o *Instrument.* A legal document.

o *Item.* Latin term, *likewise* or *also.* Often used to mark divisions or paragraphs in wills.

o *Intermarriage.* A legal term for a reciprocally agreed marriage contract.

o *Issue.* All lineal descendents, and therefore refers to more than a person's children only (e.g., grand-children, and great-grandchildren).

o *Lease.* An agreement transferring real property, usually for a specified time-period, thus creating a landlord-tenant relationship.

o *Legacy (Legatee/Legator):* A gift of personal property named in a legator's will to a legatee.

o *Legal Age.* Adulthood; under English common law: 21 for males, 18 for females.

o *Lien.* A claim by someone upon another's property as security to pay a debt.

o *Life Estate.* An estate lasting only for the life of the person given it, as in the case of a *dower* (q.v.) estate.

o *Moiety.* Half.

o *Mortgage.* A conditional title transfer of real property, as security to pay a debt. Under *common law,* the mortgagee has land possession rights; this now changed in many states.

o *Natural Affection.* Legal term found in a converyance between near relatives, when no or little money is involved; as when a parent grants property to a child.

o *Ordinary.* A jucicial probate officer in Georgia (and formerly, in South Carolina and Texas). Also refers to a hostelry where food and drink could be sold, requiring the keeper to receive an *ordinary license.* Records of the latter often found in court order books.

o *Orphan.* A minor or infant who has lost one, or both, parents.

o *Per Stipes.* A Latin term indicating the estate is divided for a group of children to be given the same share their ancestor would have received if living. Today, *by representation,* is more commonly used.

o *Petition.* A non-suit request for court action.

o *Probate.* A term originally meaning *to prove,* as in, to prove a will; by extension, now used to describe all records relating to the settling of an estate.

o *Quitrent.* A feudal term; in colonial times it usually denoted a token (similar to a tax) payment, discharging the tenant from other rents.

o *Real Property (Realty):* Land, as opposed to personal property (personalty).

o *Release.* A document giving up to another a person's right to something. A *Release of Dower,* for instance, was required to be signed by the wife whenever her husband sold property in common-law states to ensure the relinquishment of her future dower rights.

o *Relict.* Older term signifying widow or widower.

o *Separate Examination.* The legally required questioning of the wife by a court official, as in granting a deed where her dower rights must be relinquished, for instance.

o *Surety.* A person who legally promises to make good, if another defaults his obligations.

o *Surrender.* The giving up of a lease before its expiration.

o *Testate (Testator/Testatrix/Testable)/Intestate.* When a person dies leaving a valid will he is a *testator,* or *testatrix* (noun) or considered *testate* (adjective.) The opposite of the latter is

Intestate, and describes a person who didn't leave a will upon death. *Testable* means capable of making the will.

o *Testes:* Latin term for witness, sometimes abbreviated *test.*

o *Trustee:* the legal care-taker of property held *in trust* for another's benefit.

APPENDIX F. SOME CURRENT USA GENEALOGICAL PERIODICALS
(followed by year begun and where published)

Afro-American Historical and Genealogical Society, Inc. Journal. 1979 (Wash, DC)

American Genealogist. 1922 (Warwick, RI)

APG Newletter. 1979 (SLC, UT)

The Augustan. 1959 (Torrance, CA)

Bear Tracks. 1980 (SLC, UT)

British-American Genealogical Research. 1973 (McNeal, AZ)

Car-Del Scribe. 1963 (Middleboro, MA)

The Omnibus Augustan. 1967 (Torrance, CA)

DAR Magazine. 1892 (Washinton, DC)

Detroit Society for Genealogical Research Magazine. 1937 (Detroit, MI)

Families. 1971 (Ontario, Canada)

Family Fare. 1961 (Ft. Wayne, IN)

Family Puzzlers. 1964 (Danielsville, GA)

Fellowship of Brethren Genealogists Newsletter. 1968 (Elgin, IL)

The Genealogical Gazette. 1979 (Atlanta, GA)

The Genealogical Helper. 1947 (Logan, UT)

Genealogical Journal. 1972 (Salt Lake City, UT)

Genealogical Magazine of New Jersey. 1925. (New Brunswick, NJ)

The Genealogist. 1980 (NYC)

Genealogy. 1973 (Indianapolis, IN)

The Genie. 1967 (Shreveport, LA)

The German-American Genealogical Research Monographs. 1973 (McNeal, AZ)

Hereditary Register of the USA. 1972 (Wash, DC)

Illinois State Genealogical Society Quarterly. 1969 (Springfield, IL)

Je Me Souviens. 1979 (Pawtucket, RI)

Maryland and Delaware Genealogist. 1959 (St. Michaels, MD)

Names. 1953 (Berkely, CA)

National Genealogical Society Quarterly. 1912 (Wash, DC)

New England Historical and Genealogical Register. 1847 (Boston, MA)

New York Genealogical and Biographical Record. 1870 (NYC, NY)

Pennsylvania Genealogical Magazine. 1895 (Philadelphia, PA)

Prologue: Journal of the National Archives. 1969 (Wash, DC)

Ridge-Runners: a Magazine of Migration. 1972 (Ozark, MO)

Roots Digest Magazine. 1986 (SLC, UT)

Searcher. 1968 (Long Beach, CA)

St. Louis Genealogical Society Quarterly. 1968 (St. Louis, MO)

Sociedad Genealogica. 1979 (Austin, TX)

The Southern Genealogist's Exchange. 1977 (Jacksonville, FL)

Toledot: The Journal of Jewish Genealogy. 1977 (Flushing, NY)

The Trading Post. 1981 (Almagordo, NM)

Tri-State Trader. 1968 (Knightstown, IN)

Western Maryland Genealogy. 1985 (Middletown, MD)

APPENDIX G. GLOSSARY: SELECTED COMPUTER/TECHNICAL TERMS

o *Ancestral File*--A large database of family group and pedigree charts submitted mostly by LDS members and currently being computerized by the GSU.

o *Apple*--A PC company; their Apple II and Macintosh series have both been popular.

o *ASCII*--(American Standard Code for Information Exchange) The standard code used for information exchange among computer systems (see next.)

o *ASCII Text File*--A file containing only letters and numbers and a few standard format-control characters to govern things such as carriage returns. Most programs of value to genealogists can utilize ASCII files.

o *AT* An IBM model based on a powerful 80286 chip; introduced in 1984.

o *Back-up Files*--dupicate files in case the original files become damaged. These are extremely important because file damaging computer malfunctions are not uncommon.

o *Baud*--the number of bits transmitted per second. Common baud rates for the current generation of personal computer modems are 300, 1200, and 2400. We would recommend the higher rates.

o *Bit*--a contraction of Binary Digit. A bit can either be a 0 or a 1, and is the smallest unit of information in a binary system. Eight bits are used to make up a byte which represents a letter or a number.

o *Boolean*--a type of formal logic formulated by George Boole and used in information retrieval to specify a search through the use of words such as AND, OR, and NOT. Let's say, for example, you want pieces of information dealing with Smiths who married Joneses but not Joneses who lived in New York. The Boolean search command: Search Smith AND (Jones NOT New York) would retrieve only pieces of information containing the names SMITH and JONES, but not those Joneses associated with NEW YORK.

o *Bug*--A programming error or malfunction. Many of these are not detected until after the program has been released to the public. All programs have bugs, for this reason new releases are continually being produced with added features and known "bugs" removed.

o *Bulletin Board (BB)*--A computer accessible by telephone line; with proper authorization, you can read, and/or add to, messages and directories (a directory of free software, for example).

o *Byte*--a sequence of adjacent bits which often represent a letter or a digit. Think of a byte as being one character, such as the letter "a."

o *Central Processing Unit (CPU)*--the controlling electronics behind the computer, or chip(s) that makes the system go.

o *Chip*--a small electronic device containing an integrated circuit package usually on a wafer of silicon. Thousands of transitors may be contained in one "chip."

o *Clone*--an almost identical copy of an original.

o *COM (Computer Output Microfiche)*--Microfiche (q.v.) output of an online database.

o *Compatible*--usually a computer made to run software designed for a well-known personal computer, such as the Apple II or the IBM-PC. As no computer, to our knowledge, is 100 percent compatible, make sure before purchase that a machine claiming compatibility actually does run the software of your interest.

o *CompuServe*--Commercial on-line information center available by subscription.

o *Computer*--an electronic machine which can do numerous complex arithmetic or logical operations during a run without needing human intervention.

o *Copy-Protection*--to prevent illegal copying some software has been fixed, i.e., copy-protected, so as to make it almost impossible to make another copy (or, in some cases, to make more than one working copy).

o *CP/M*--An operating system (q.v.) that was quite popular, and supported a number of various computers. Now outmoded in that these systems are limited to only 64 K, and not compatible with the present-day de facto MS-DOS standard.

o *Cursor*--a movable spot of light on the computer or terminal's screen that indicates where the next character will be entered.

o *Daisy-Wheel Printer*--a printer using a round disk containing a set of one type font.

o *Database Program*--a program designed to manipulate data (numbers or words). Generally, the data is stored in fields, and the fields comprise a record, and the records comprise a file. The records may be searched and sorted, and the and fields in the selected records may be output as reports.

o *Disk Drive*--Diskette drive. The device which turns the disk or diskette, transferring data from the files on the disk or diskette to the computer's memory and visa versa.

o *Diskette*--Floppy disk. A flat, circular sheet of flexible mylar coated with a magnetic oxide, rotating inside a square protective jacket which continuously cleans the surface. Files can be copied on to it or read off of it into the computer's memory.

o *DOS (Disk Operating System)* software which controls the execution of computer programs and acts as kind of a housekeeper between the computer, the keyboard, the monitor, etc.

o *Dot-Matrix Printer*--a printer using a printhead with from 9 to 24 pins. Combinations of the pins hitting the paper produce patterns (fonts or graphics).

o *DSDD (Double-sided, double-density)*--a common flopppy diskette format using both sides and allowing for more data storage than is possible on a single-sided, single-density (SSSD) diskette.

o *Export*--To send a file of information from one computer program to another.

o *Fido/Fidonet*--the latter an international bulletin board system of some 1,200 nodes using *Fido*, a shareware bulletin board program.

o *Freeware*--software made available to other computer users at no charge. These programs are readily available on computer bulletin boards and from computer clubs.

o *Function Key*--A computer key usually designated with the letter "F." Rather than printing a character on the screen, it performs some predefined function, depending on the program instructions.

o *GEDCOM (GEnealogical Data COmmunications*--An input/output format being developed by the GSU to standardize genealogical telecommunications and exchange.

o *GEnie (GE Network for Information Exchange)*--Commercial on-line information center available by subscription.

GIGO (Garbage In, Garbage Out)--computer jargon meaning that if bad data goes into the system, only bad data can come out.

o *Hardcopy*--The printed results of a computer file.

o *Hard Disk*--a disk composed of a magnetic coating applied to a rigid substrate. Hard disks are generally faster and have more storage than diskettes or floppy disks. Common sizes for now are 10, 20, 40 or 60 megabytes; Manufacturers are pushing into the multiple hundreds of megabytes range. The upper limits on hard disk capacity don't appear to have been reached. Hard disks vary in quality; some are apt to "crash," and lose valuable data. Always make duplicate files of those stored on both hard and floppy disks.

o *Hardware*--physical computer equipment, as opposed to computer programs which are termed software.

o *IBM PC*--Name brand of a "Personal Computer" made by the IBM Company.

o *Import*--to bring a file of data from one computer program into another.

o *Integrated Software Package*--One in which the same data can be used between the different programs; (e.g., names and addresses taken from a word processor, and put into a database program, or a mail-merge program).

o *K*--1024 bytes. A computer's memory and function are measured by number of K's.

o *Keyboard*--An input device; resembles a typewriter keyboard.

o *Laptop*--small-sized, portable computers; weighing usually from 5-15 pounds.

Laser Printer--a printer in which a laser beam produces an image which rolls off a drum in a similar fashion to a photocopy machine.

o *GSU*--Genealogical Society of Utah

o *Macintosh*--A computer put out by the Apple Company

o *Megabyte (MB)*--A measuring unit equal to 1,000 bytes (q.v.)

o *Memory*--This term usually refers to the computer memory, or that area in the computer where data is temporarily stored and manipulated. Most personal computers have both random access memory (*RAM*) and read only memory (*ROM*). *RAM* memory can be manipulated, while *ROM* memory was installed in the factory and contains programs and instructions which cannot be changed.

o *Microfiche*--rectangular pieces of film containing text and graphic data.

o *Microfilm*--text and graphic data copied onto rolls of film for preservation.

o *Modem (MOdulator-DEModulator)*-- A device that converts the digital (on-off) signals of the computer to the modulating signals of the telephone lines and visa versa. Both sender and receiver must have modems to communicate.

o *Monitor*--A cathode ray tube (CRT) device which serves as the computer's screen. Similiar to a television screen.

o *MS-DOS PC*: Acronym for MicroSoft Disk Operating System (q.v.); IBM-compatible

o *National Genealogical Conference (NGC)*--a part of *Fidonet* (q.v.), especially set up for genealogical use.

o *Node*--one communications computer in a computer network.

o OCR--Acronym for "Optical character recognition" (q.v.).

o *Online*--A computer system where the user can interact with the computer. All current personal computers are online systems.

o *Operating System (OS)*-- See *DOS*

o *Optical Character Recognition (OCR)*--The machine identification of printed characters through use of light-sensitive devices.

o *OS/2*--An Operating System being developed by IBM and by Microsoft to support '286 and '386 (the next generation of) PC's.

o *Parallel*--Input/output connections with 8 wires and so able to transmit all 8 bits of a byte simultaneously. Compare to: *Serial* input/output connections that send the 8 bits one after another.

o *PC*--Personal Computer; can be a generic term, or else refers to a model manufactured by IBM.

o *PC-DOS*: Acronym for Personal Computer (the IBM registered) Disk Operating System (q.v.)

o *Port*--A place on the computer where a cable can connect the computer with other hardware options; it can be either a *Parallel* or *Serial* port (q.v.).

o *Printer*--An output device that converts bytes to readable characters on paper.

o *Proximity Operators*--Symbols used in information retrieval informing the computer that the words you are searching for must be adjacent to each other or in some other physical relationship to each other, e.g. in the same field. (See also *Boolean*.)

o *Public-Domain Software*--Non-copyrighted software.

o *RAM*--See *Memory*

o *ROM*--See *Memory*

o *Scanner*--an optical device which reads a pattern from a printed page and puts it into a form which the computer can store.

o *Shareware*--software which is freely distributed but which if used on a continual basis the author expects renumeration. The philosophy here is "try it, and if you like it, please pay." Much of the shareware is excellent, and lower in price than software marketed in the tradition manner.

o *SIG*--Special Interest Group; usually a sub-group of a Computer User Group

o *Software*--computer programs as opposed to *hardware*, or computer equipment.

o *Software Librarian*--in a computer user group, the person in charge of the group's software.

o *Soundex*--a name index based on the sound of the name rather than spelling.

o *The Source*--Commerical on-line information center available by subscription.

o *Sysop*--Systems Operator, or the person controlling and operating a given bulletin board mode.

o *Support*--Technical and/or other kinds of help and encouragement needed by beginners in computers.

o *Telecommunications*--communicating over long distances by telephone, or some other means. These communications may be voice, numbers or text, or pictures.

o *Teleconferencing System*--a system whereby people at various geographical locations may take part in the same conference.

o *Tiny-Tafel*—a computer-genealogy format containing names, places and time-periods of interest, and used to upload that data onto the *NGC* (q.v.).

o *User-Friendly*—easy to learn and to use.

o *User-Group*—An organization based upon using computers, or a particular kind of computer or software.

o *Word Processor*—A computer program allowing for addition or revision or subtraction of text, so as to obtain "perfect" copy. Excellent for storing genealogical notes, writing letters, etc.

o *Worm* (*Write Once, Read Many*)—A form of optical disk technology allowing the user to record (but not revise) and store large amounts of data economically on a small disk or cartridge.

o *Write Protection*—the little notch on the diskette is covered to prevent accidentally writing to, or otherwise changing, the original disk contents.

o *XT*—An older IBM model based on the 8088 chip; limited to 640K RAM.

APPENDIX H. FORMS: Pedigree Chart (p. 119) & Family Group Chart (p. 120)
developed by Genealogical Society, Church of Jesus Christ of Latter-day Saints; uncopyrighted.

Family Group Record

Page ___ of ___

LDS ORDINANCE DATA
B - Baptized   E - Endowed
S - Sealed to spouse   P - Sealed to parents

Husband's name

			Date	Temple
Born	Place	B		
Chr.	Place	E		
Mar.	Place	S		
Died	Place	P		
Bur.	Place			

Father	Mother

Husband's other wives

Wife's name

			Date	Temple
Born	Place	B		
Chr.	Place	E		
Died	Place	P		
Bur.	Place			

Father	Mother

Wife's other husbands

Children   List each child (whether living or dead) in order of birth

			Date	Temple

1 Sex | Name   Spouse

			Date	Temple
Born	Place	B		
Chr.	Place	E		
Mar.	Place	S		
Died	Place	P		

2 Sex | Name   Spouse

Born	Place	B		
Chr.	Place	E		
Mar.	Place	S		
Died	Place	P		

3 Sex | Name   Spouse

Born	Place	B		
Chr.	Place	E		
Mar.	Place	S		
Died	Place	P		

4 Sex | Name   Spouse

Born	Place	B		
Chr.	Place	E		
Mar.	Place	S		
Died	Place	P		

☐ Check here if additional children are listed on reverse side.

Additional Information

Record on the back:
- Sources of information
- Other marriages, sealings, and explanations

Check the box for one of the following options (applies to all names submitted on this form):

☐ **OPTION 1— FAMILY FILE** Send all names to my family file at the _____
Temple. I will provide proxies for: ☐ Baptism ☐ Endowment ☐ Sealing
I understand that ordinances not checked will have proxies assigned by the temple.

☐ **OPTION 2 — TEMPLE FILE** Send all names to any temple and assign proxies for all approved ordinances.

☐ **OPTION 3 — ANCESTRAL FILE** Send all names to the Ancestral File. (You must include a pedigree chart or required form.) No ordinances will be done.

Name and address of person submitting form

Phone ( )	Date prepared
Stake/Mission	Stake/Mission unit no.

Relationship of above to:

Husband_____ Wife_____

Published by The Church of Jesus Christ of Latter-day Saints   PFGS3107   3/87   Printed in USA

(left margin) Write places as: Tryon, Polk, NC   or   St. Martins, Birmingham, Warwick, Eng.

(left margin) Write name as: Robert Thomas MEYERS
Write date as: 4 Oct 1986

Husband's name

Wife's name

CHILDREN List each child (whether living or dead) in order of birth

				Date	Temple
5 Sex	Name		Spouse		
	Born	Place		B	
	Chr.	Place		E	
	Mar.	Place		S	
	Died	Place		P	
6 Sex	Name		Spouse		
	Born	Place		B	
	Chr.	Place		E	
	Mar.	Place		S	
	Died	Place		P	
7 Sex	Name		Spouse		
	Born	Place		B	
	Chr.	Place		E	
	Mar.	Place		S	
	Died	Place		P	
8 Sex	Name		Spouse		
	Born	Place		B	
	Chr.	Place		E	
	Mar.	Place		S	
	Died	Place		P	

☐ Check here if additional children are listed on another Family Group Record and attach the record to this form. Include parents' names.

Sources of information (add further information on attached sheets as necessary)

Other marriages, sealings, and necessary explanations (add further information on attached sheets as necessary)

☐ Check here if any female listed on this form was sealed to another husband **in her lifetime.** (Give details below.)

Please note:
When using this form to submit names for temple ordinances or to the Ancestral File, only you can ensure that the information is as *accurate* and *complete* as practical. Please take every reasonable step to see that this happens. This will help maintain the integrity of Church genealogical files and reduce duplication of temple ordinance work.

INDEX (Note: Many legal & technical terms defined in Appendixes are not indexed)

— A —

Abbreviations & punctuation, 96
Abstracting, a useful technique, 18
Accuracy, 7, 36, 47, 58
Accredited researchers, 108
Addresses & address sources: See Chapter 15
Africa, 90, 102
Ages, determining from clues, 56-7, 59, 95
AIS Indexes, 15, 38, 81, 90
Alabama, 50, 72, 79, 81
Alaska, 72, 79
Albania, 102
American & British Genealogy & Heraldry, 48, 51-3
American (USA) research, 12, 38, 48, 56-8, 61-2,
    64-5, 68-9, 71-2, 73-4, 77, 79, 83, 92-3, 98; See
    also: AIS Indexes; Civil/Rev. War; Colonial USA
Analysis, necessary in research, 56-8, 61-2
Ancestral File, 15-6, 39
Andereck, Paul, Computer-genealogist, 32
Anglican Church (Established; Episcopal), 73-4, 76
Annex, store for family album supplies, 9-10
Apple computer, 28, 31, 33,
Arizona, 72, 79, 95
Archives, 41, 71, 73, 110
Arkansas, 72, 79, 81
Asia, 12, 70, 103
askSAM software, 27
AT computer, 26
Austria, 12, 69, 84
— B —
Baltic States, 102
Baptist records, 74
Baud, speed rate in telecommunications, 34
Belgium, 105
Bible records, 51, 54
Bibliographies & indexes, 43, 48-9, 50-2
Birth-order, 57
Black-out period in USA research, 38
Black research, 69, 70, 90, 92
Bookstores, 101
Boston Transcript, microfilmed collection, 50
Boundary problems, 12, 64
Branch genealogical libraries, 11, 14, 37, 82
British research, 12, 44, 49, 51, 69, 90, 92, 105
Bulgaria, 102
Burial records, See: Cemetery & burial records
— C —
California, 14, 34-5, 41, 72, 79, 80-1, 95, 99
Calendar changes, 57, 111
Call numbers, 42
Cameras, useful in recording, 9

Canada, 12, 45, 51, 66, 69, 70, 80, 88, 98-9, 102
C-PAF UG, 33
Card and electronic catalogs, 13, 41
Catholic records, 66-7, 73
CD-ROM, 13, 26, 33, 45
Cemetery & burial records, 74-5
Censuses & indexes, 15, 59, 60-2, 65-6, 79, 80-2, 85
Central Europe, 12
Certified researchers, 108
Chinese, 86, 90, 103; See also: Asia
Choosing line(s) to research; See Chapter 5
Christenings, 71
Church of Jesus Christ of Latter-day Saints
    See LDS Church; GSU
Church records, 56, 61, 66, 73-4, 76, 97-8
City Directories, 44
Civil War (& Confederate) records, 37, 81, 83
Colonial USA, 49, 73, 77, 84
Colorado, 34, 41, 72, 79
COM (Computer-Output-Microfiche), 11-16, 80
Common law, English, 95
Common names, 21, 40
CommSoft, 29, 35
Communist countries, 64, 102-3
Compiled sources, Chapter 7, 39, 43, 45-6, 78, 83-4
Compuserve, database & info center, 27, 30
Computerized genealogy, See Chapter 4
Conferences & seminars, 49, 99
Conflicting data, 55
Connecticut, 65, 72, 85
Correspondence, 19, 73, 77, 84, 97, 106-7
County clerks, working with, 77, 84, 97, 106-7
Court records, 77-8
Cousin, definition has varied, 94
Cross-indexing, to record same data on many, 20
Cuba, 102
Czechosovakia & Slovak, 70, 102
— D —
Dating & chronology, 56-7, 95, Appendix C
Daughters of American Revolution(DAR), 58, 79, 83, 100
Delaware, 34-5, 72, 77, 80-1, 87
Denmark, 104
Dialog, 45
Direct line, definition of, 7
Discrepancy table for conflicting facts, 55
Dissertation Abstracts, 45
Ditto, use & abbreviation of, 96
Documentation/Document file, 8, 17, 20
Dollarhide, W., computers/geography, 28, 31, 65
Duplication, how to avoid, 39
Dutch/Netherlands research, 69, 73, 88, 90, 92, 94, 106

— E —

Eakle, Arlene H., 21, 53
Eastern Europe, 86
English research, 12,44,48-9,51,57,60,69-70,82-4,
    86-7,92,99,105; See also: Common Law, English
Ethnic genealogy; 14, 39, 69, 70; See also:
    Black research, Jewish research, etc.,
Europe, 69, 93
Evidence, 10, 53-6, 58, 76

— F —

Family Album, making one, 10
Family Folders, 19
Family Group Charts, 7, 18, 120
Family histories, 47, 51-2
Family myths/skeletons, 38
Family Registry of GSU, 14, 16, 39
Family Reunions, provide good opportunities, 9
Family Roots software, 33
Family traditions, 10, 63
Federation of Family History Societies in UK (FFHSUK),
    49, 105
Fidonet, computer BB network, 35
Filby, P. Wm., author, 48, 51, 53, 87-8
Finding tools, See Chapter 10; 60, 68, 80, 86, 90
Finland, 104
First names, 90-2
Florida, 34-5, 72, 79, 80-1, 97, 105
Forms, 7, 82, Appendix H
France, 84, 94, 97, 105

— G —

GEDCOM, telecommunication format, 16, 29, 30
Genealogical Helper (Everton), 48, 98, 101
Genealogical Information System (GIS), 11, 15-6, 81
Genealogical Library of Salt Lake, See GSU
Genealogical Library Catalog (GLC), 13
Genealogical & Local History Books in Print, 43
Genealogical Research, 53, 69
Genealogical Research Directory, 39
Genealogy on Display, genealogy shareware, 31
GEnie, commercial BB, 34
Gentlemen, a social class term, 92
Geography, 12; See also Chapter 10;search services,64,101
Georgia, 72, 77, 80-1, 83, 101
Gerhan, J. D., software developer, 28
Germany (& german-speaking groups), 12, 29, 47,
    64-6, 70, 73, 84, 86-7, 90, 92-3, 96-8, 102
GIGO, 36
Greece, 103
GSU (and holdings): 45, 51, 66, 73, 77, 81, 86, 107;
    See also: Chapter 2 & Appendix H
Guide to Genealogical Research in the National Archives,
    79, 83-4
Guidebooks, 65-6, 69-70, 79

— H —

Haley, Alex, author, 9, 11

Handwriting, 96
Handy Book, 64, 73, 77, 79, 98, 107
Heritage Quest, 44, 49
Headstones, See Tombstones
Hispanic research, 70, 82, 90
Historical Abstracts, 45
Historical background, 65
Hungary, 12, 103

— I —

IBM (and clone) computers, 25-6, 33
Iceland, 104
Idaho, 14, 72, 79, 95
Identification, means of, 91-2
IGI, 12-13, 39, 86, 90
Illinois, 50, 72, 79, 81, 100
Image Enhancement technology, 82
Immigrant America, by Thomas Sowell, 90
Immigration/Naturalization, 44, 79, 84-6
Indentured servants, 39
Indexes, 42, See also: Bibliographies; Censuses
Index Publishing, 80-1
Indian research, See Native American research
Indian Wars, 83
Indiana, 35, 69, 72, 79, 93, 99, 101
Information Storage, Mass, progress in, 45-6
Inheritance, 77, 79
In-law vs step-, 94
Inter-library loan (ILL), 14, 44, 49, 101
International Genealogical Index, See: IGI
Iowa, 35, 72, 79
Ireland/Irish, 70, 74-5, 86-7, 90-1, 105
Israel, 104
Italy, 90, 97, 105

— J —

Jacobus, Donald, Genealogist, 39, 53
Japan/Japanese, 90, 103
Jewish research, 29, 69, 70, 90, 104
Johnson, Arta, German expert, 96
Johnson, P. G., western VA historian, 53
Journals, 10
Junior, an age designation, 92, 94
Jurisdictions, 66-7, 71, 78-9

— K —

Kansas, 72, 79, 81-2
Kegley's VA Frontier, good compiled source, 53
Kentucky, 41, 65, 72, 78, 80-1
Knowledge Index, 34, 45
KUGIG, 33

— L —

Land records, 61, 66, 78-80
Language of immigrant as locality clue, 59
Language problems, 37, 89, 94, 95
Latin American research, 12, 70, 102
Law of primogeniture, 67
LDS Church: 5, 7, 11-2, 28, 73, 96, 99

Librarians/Libraries, See:Chapter 6; 41-6,98,106
Library of Congress, 45, 79, 99
Local genealogy/history societies,48-9,66,68-9,98
Local histories, 48, 64
Locality Catalog of GSU, 13-4,38,63,66,73,78-9,82
Louisiana, 71-2, 79, 81, 95
Lutheran records, 61-2, 73
Luxemburg, 105

— M —

Macintosh computer, 28
Maine, 72, 78, 85
Map & atlas sources, 63-65, 67-68
Marriage records, 54,57,71-2,73,95; See also: Vital
Marquis' *Who's Who*, 45
Maryland, 34, 52, 64, 72, 77, 90, 85, 88, 99, 101
Massachusetts, 34, 44, 72, 78, 85, 90, 99, 101
Memory & storage in computers, 25-6
Methodist records, 74
Mexico/Mexican War, 12, 51, 79, 83, 102
Michigan, 72, 79, 81, 99, 101
Microfiche & Microfilm collections, 11, 44, 49, 50, 67,
    73, 77; See also: GSU & National Archives
Midwestern States, periodical for, 101
Migration & Migration patterns, 38, 64, 80
Military records, 79, 83-4, 91
Minnesota, 72, 79
Miscellaneous files, 21
Mississippi, 72, 79, 81
Missouri, 72, 79, 81
Mistaken identity and common names, 21, 40
Monaco, 106
Montana, 72, 79
Moravian records, 73
Mormon records, 73; at BYU, 99; See also: GSU
Mortician records, 74-5
Mrs., formerly a social class term, 94
My Roots software, 28

— N —

Name Extraction Program of GSU, 11, 15, 16
Names/Naming Patterns, 12, 14, 21, 40, 56, 63, 65,
    89-94, 98; See Also: Surnames; First names
National Archives & branches, 44, 79, 81-4, 100
Nat'l Genealogical Society (NGS), 14, 33-5, 100, 108
National Genealogical Conference (NGC), 34-5
Native American research, 39, 70
Naturalization/Immigration, 60, 66, 79, 84-6
Nebraska, 35, 41, 72, 79
Nephew & niece, definition has varied, 94
Nevada, 72, 79, 81, 95
Newberry Library, Chicago, 50, 100
New England Historic Genealogical Soc., 49,51,100
New England states, 12, 35, 37, 51, 69, 73, 77, 87, 95
New Hampshire, 72, 85
New Jersey, 71-2, 77, 80, 85, 87
New Mexico, 72, 79, 95

Newspapers, 49, 52
New York, 17, 34-5, 43-4, 50-1, 59, 64-5, 72, 77-8, 82
    85, 87, 100-1
NGS CIG, 32-4
Nicknames, 91
North Carolina, 14, 65, 72-3, 77-8, 81
North Dakota, 72, 79
Notetaking & Notekeeping, See Chapter 3
NPR (National Projects Registry), 34
Norway, 104

— O —

Occupation, as genealogical clue, 79, 89, 90
Offline databases, 46
Ohio, 34-5, 72, 79, 81, 100
Oklahoma, 41, 72, 79, 81
One Hundred (100) Most Used Books, 16, 43
Online searching, 34, 44-5
Optical disks/scanners & OCR, 26-7
Oral genealogies/interviewing principles, 5,9,11
Oregon, 72, 79, 80-1
Organization, See Recording
Original records, 11, 13, 71, 92, 96
Ortssippenbucher, 47

— P —

Patriarch software, 79
Patronymics, 12, 89
Parish and Vital Records Listings, 13
Passenger lists, See Immigration records
PC-Write, 31
Pedigree Charts, 7, 18, 119
Pence, Richard, genealogy author/editor, 32
Pennsylvania, 35, 64-5, 72, 77, 81, 86-8, 101
Pension records, See Military records
Periodicals, 32, 49, 52, Appendix F
Personal Ancestral File (PAF) software, 16, 28
Phonebooks, source of relative addresses, 98
Philippines, 103
Photocopy, 18, 44, 77
Placenames, 63
Platte bookes, 80
Poland, 97, 103
Port cities suspect as birthplace, 63
Portugal, 106
Posey, Joanna, computer-genealogist, 32
Power of attorney records, 80
Pratt, David, BYU genealogy instructor, 39
Price-to-power ratio, 26, 36
Primogeniture, 77
Probate records, See Wills & probates
Processioning records, 76
ProComm, 34
Professional genealogists, lists of, 108
Public Domain land, 79
Public-domain software, 30
Publishers, 101

Publishing your genealogy, 26, 109
Punctuation, See: Abbreviations & punctuation
        --- Q ---
QUG, 33
Q-Modem, 34
Quakers, 73, 75, 86
Quinsept, 28, 33
        --- R ---
Record destruction, 37
Recording/Record-keeping helps, 8, 17-21, 36, 98
Relatives, 8-9,18,37,43,45,58,62,74,80,106
Research agenda, 20, 26, 60, 62
Research Aids, GSU, 14-5, 66, 79, 87
Research repositories, 41, 98-100
Revolutionary War & RW era, 38, 54, 65, 73, 83
Rhode Island, 72, 77, 80-1, 85
Rights of Privacy laws, 8-9, 81
Romania, 97, 103
Roots II software, 26, 28-9, 34-5
Royalty, desire to be related to, 39
Rubincam, Milton R., author, 53, 69
Russia/Russian Empire, 64, 84, 103
        --- S ---
Salt Lake Distribution Center, 15, 28
Salt Lake Library, See GSU
SASE = Self-addressed, stamped envelope
Scandinavia, 12, 99, 104
Schweitzer, George K., author, 65, 69, 101
Scotland/Scotch research, 70,75,82,87,90,106
Senior, age designation, 92, 94
Service records, See Military records
Shareware, 30-1
Shreiner-Yantis, Nellie, 43, 51
Signatures, marks, brands to identify, 92
Slave names to trace black/white descent, 92
Social desirability as research factor, 39
Societies, 48, 50, 67
Software, 27-32
Soundex Index, 27, 81
South Carolina, 41, 65, 72, 77, 80-1, 88, 101
South Dakota, 72, 79
Southern Europe, poorly represented on IGI, 12
Southern States, 12, 37, 51, 73, 75, 87
Spain/Spanish research, 82, 95, 105
Spelling only recently standardized; check for variants
        14, 63, 89, 93-4
Stagecoach Library Bulletin, 50
State Archives, 41, 71, 82
Step-child/parent, 94
Summary sheet, 20, 62
Surname Catalog of GSU, 13
Surnames, 12, 15, 75, 82, 89, 92-3; See also: Names
Sweden, 70, 86, 104
Switzerland, 12, 70

        --- T ---
Tape and/or video recorders, 9
Targetted approach for thorough research, 42-3
Tax lists, 80, 95
Telecommunications, 29-30, 34-5, 37, 97
Tennessee, 14, 65, 72, 77, 79, 80-1
Tepper, Michael, Editor, 87
Texas, 14, 34, 41, 79, 81, 95
The Source, 53, 66, 74, 78, 86, 96
The Source, database & info center, 30
Thorndale, census-maps, 65
Tiny-Tafel, 35
Tithable lists = tax lists, 95
Tombstones, 75
Topography, 64
        --- U ---
User groups, 31, 33
User-supported programs, 30-1
Utah, 34, 72, 79, 99, 101; See also: GSU
        --- V ---
Vermont, 49, 71-2, 78-9
Virginia, 12, 14, 34, 37, 49, 52-3, 55, 57, 72-3
        76-8, 80-1, 84, 95, 101
Video-tape recorder, 9
Vital records, 13, 53, 71-2, 76, 92, 95; (See also:
        Bible/Marriage/Cemetery/Christening/Original records;
        Microform collections)
Vocabulary, for computers, 24, Appendix G
        --- W ---
Wales, 12, 69, 82
War of 1812, 83
Washington, 41, 72, 79, 95
Washington, DC, 79-81, 99, 100
West Virginia, 12-4, 72, 78, 81
Whole Earth Software Catalog, 27, 32
Wills & probates, 57, 66, 77-8
Wisconsin, 72, 79
Women, record-keeping status, 95
World War 1 draft records, 83
Wyoming, 72, 79, 81
        --- X, Y, Z ---
XT (and Clones) Computers, 25-6, 36
Yugoslavia, 97, 103
ZyIndex, 27

Pedigree Chart

Chart number _____

Number 1 on this chart is the same as no. _____ on chart no. _____

Mark (X) boxes when ordinances are completed.
- B = Baptized
- E = Endowed
- S = Sealed to spouse
- P = Sealed to parents
- F = Family group record (Mark [X] this box when this person appears on a family group record as a parent.)
- C = Children's ordinances completed (Mark [X] this box when all ordinances are completed for all children of this couple.)

St. Martins, Birmingham, Warwick, Eng.

Write places as: Tryon, Polk, NC or

8 (Father of #4) B E S P F C   Cont. on chart _____
Born/Chr
Place
Married
Place
Died
Place

4 (Father of #2) B E S P F C
Born/Chr
Place
Married
Place
Died
Place

9 (Mother of #4) B E S P F C   Cont. on chart _____
Born/Chr
Place
Died
Place

2 (Father of #1) B E S P F C
Born/Chr
Place
Married
Place
Died
Place

10 (Father of #5) B E S P F C   Cont. on chart _____
Born/Chr
Place
Married
Place
Died
Place

5 (Mother of #2) B E S P F C
Born/Chr
Place
Died
Place

11 (Mother of #5) B E S P F C   Cont. on chart _____
Born/Chr
Place
Died
Place

1 B E S P F C
Born/Chr
Place
Married
Place
Died
Place

(Spouse of #1) B E S P F C

12 (Father of #6) B E S P F C   Cont. on chart _____
Born/Chr
Place
Married
Place
Died
Place

6 (Father of #3) B E S P F C
Born/Chr
Place
Married
Place
Died
Place

13 (Mother of #6) B E S P F C   Cont. on chart _____
Born/Chr
Place
Died
Place

3 (Mother of #1) B E S P F C
Born/Chr
Place
Died
Place

Write name as: Robert Thomas MEYERS
Write dates as: 4 Oct 1986

14 (Father of #7) B E S P F C   Cont. on chart _____
Born/Chr
Place
Married
Place
Died
Place

7 (Mother of #3) B E S P F C
Born/Chr
Place
Died
Place

15 (Mother of #7) B E S P F C   Cont. on chart _____
Born/Chr
Place
Died
Place

Person Submitting Pedigree Chart

Name

Address

Telephone number
(   )

Date prepared

Published by The Church of Jesus Christ of Latter-day Saints

(8½" × 11", with ordinance boxes) PFGS3093 2·87 Printed in USA

ORDER FORM

Please send the services or products check-marked below:

TURBO GENEALOGY, 1987/88 edition ($17.95 enclosed). [ ]

1987/88 *Update* ($4.95 enclosed). [ ] (32 pages of new material added since the 1986 edition of: *Climb it Right--a high-tech genealogical primer*, predecessor of *TURBO GENEALOGY*)

Free information re: the *Virginia Genealogical Databank* [ ]

Computer-Genealogy software reviews; ($1.50 each, or $5 for all)

   (a) *Personal Ancestral File (PAF)*, version 2 [ ]

   (b) *Roots II*, version 2 by Commsoft [ ]

   (c) *Family Roots*, version 3 by Quinsept [ ]

   (d) *My Roots* by Mark Peters [ ]

(The latter two reviews available July, 1987.)

On behalf of the _____ Genealogical Society, we request your *free* genealogical columns. Enclosed is an SASE. (Tell us if you have already received some of these so we don't duplicate your back issues.)

[ ] Check here if you have friends/relatives who may want to learn more about our books and services; then write their names on the back.

[ ] Check here if you have updated or helpful genealogical information that you think should be included in our next edition; or for any content errors detected. Describe these in detail on the reverse, and return as soon as possible. We reserve all rights as to what is acceptable, but if we agree with your judgment, you will automatically receive a free copy of the next edition or update.

TOTAL:
(Please make your check payable to PROGENESYS PRESS. FREE SHIPPING; or, for optional air-mail delivery, add $2.50. Virginia residents add 4 1/2% sales tax [81c per book; or 22c per booklet, or per package of four software reviews].)

Name:

Street Address:

Town, State, Zip:

Phone (include area code):

Mail with payment to: *Progenesys Press*, PO Box 2623, Christiansburg, VA 24068-2623

(Photocopy this order form if you like.)

ABOUT THE AUTHORS

John Cosgriff is a reference librarian and online science researcher at Virginia Tech, having received his M.L.S. at Brigham Young University. Since 1981 he been involved in computer-genealogy, first as a learner, than as a teacher, author, lecturer, and, more recently, as a columnist and software reviewer. His wife and co-author, Carolyn Cosgriff, has concurrently headed a computer-genealogy firm specializing in Virginia. They are native Californians with undergraduate degrees from U.C., Berkeley and Stanford University respectively. Their seven children are active in art, sports (track, soccer and gymnastics), Scouts, and dance when not attending school in their home-town, Christiansburg, Virginia.

4   12/19/88